I thought I'd beg
some of the many
from readers evel
words and feeling
chord in your heart!

_____ a responsive

"I bought your book on Saturday afternoon and read it the same evening non-stop."
Gary Johnson, *Mail Carrier*

"The book was wonderful. My husband and I were going to Washington via Amtrak, and I was so wrapped up in it, I almost made us miss the train."
Helene Breedlove, *Church Educator*

"I haven't read a book all the way through in thirty years, but I couldn't put yours down."
Jim F. Brown, *Business Consultant*

"Though I had gone into the bookstore for another book, yours seemed to jump out at me, and am I glad it did. I stay at home with two small children, but somehow, I managed to read your book in one sitting!"
Angie Shubert: *Full-time Mother*

"Your book reads like a modern Paul. I praise God for you my friend." **Cecil Williamson,** *Evangelist*

"Your book is a living portrait of evangelism. It will convert people by itself if only the unsaved would read it. It is so alive, moving, convincing and compelling. Thank God for Ron Levin!"
Bishop William R. Cannon
Former President: The World Methodist Council

more . . .

i

"So few have experienced real Christian awakening. Brother, tell it loud, tell it clear, and tell it often!"
Vergil Scott, *Bookstore owner*

"Southern Bell can hang it up. Your book has reached out and touched someone.' God love your heart."
Dianne Cown, *Cosmetologist*

"Dear Ron, your book not only strengthened my faith, it set me on fire."
Pam Williams, *Working mother*

"As I was reading (rapidly, because it was so wonderful) you opened up a whole new world of trusting God for me. Your story shows me how He is in control. See you in heaven!"
Ruth Anne Harley, *Homemaker*

"Thank you for sharing so much of what God has done through you. I am 28 years old and just wanted to let you know that your book has given me a renewed hope and hunger and also a peace. God be with you."
Erin Suttles, *A Searching Young Soul*

"I kissed my husband goodbye for a business trip on Monday and that night he called at 12:15 and encouraged me to go to sleep. I had been reading your book. At 1:30 I was still awake, reading, and stayed up til I finished it. I loved your story!"
Linda Clark, *Training Specialist*

"Just finished reading your book with tears in our eyes and an overflowing heart. What a treasure you are for those who know the Lord, as well as those who *need* to know Him."
Kerry & Jean Clippard
Furniture retailers

"Brilliant, masterful, vigorously written. This is one of the most thrilling stories of conversion I have ever read."
Bishop Earl Hunt
Holder: World Methodism Chair of Honor

"I have read your book, then re-read parts of it again. I am 86 years young and have been a Christian since April, 1920. I can't wait to give my pastor a copy to read."
Mrs. L. W. New, Jr.

"I stayed up late and arose early so I could finish your book. It made me laugh, cry, think and pray. Reading it also got me thinking about my own personal relation-ship with our Lord."
Ellen Mills, *Working mom*

"A passionate story. One cannot turn the pages fast enough. Ron, thank you for sharing yourself with us so completely. This is a book that everyone should read."
Bishop James S. Thomas
Candler School of Theology

"A few days have passed now, and I'm over the tears I shed reading your book. It was wonderful and compel-ling and kept me wanting more and more. Thanks for helping me to understand that when times get tough, we are never really alone. He is there!"
Diana Murtha, *Surgical nurse*

"I could not stop reading until I was finished. What a powerful book. May God continue to use you and your talents for the work that is much needed today.
P.S. Bernice, my wife, could not put it down either."
Monroe Turner, *Business Executive*

iii

The Long Journey Home

THE STORY OF A JEW'S MODERN-DAY PILGRIMAGE TO CHRIST

Ron Levin

Library of Congress Catalog Card Number: 94-76014

Second Printing: January 1995
Published by Ron Levin Ministries
4303 Old Greenville Highway
Liberty, SC 29657   803-646-6425

PRINTED IN THE UNITED STATES OF AMERICA
Faith Printing, Taylors, SC 29687

ISBN 0-9640720-0-9

**Dedicated to the memory
of my father, Meyer Levin.**

*Perhaps he knew more than
he was ever able to tell us.*

But now, this is what the LORD says —
he who created you, O Jacob,
he who formed you, O Israel:
"Fear not, for I have redeemed you;
I have summoned you by name;
you are mine." *Isaiah 43:1*

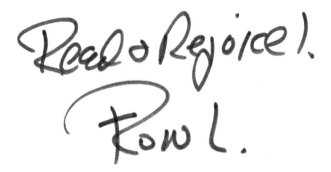

IN GRATEFUL ACKNOWLEDGEMENT

For Jack, who was there when I needed him.
For Reuben, who accompanied me through hell.
For Jim Thomas, my bishop . . . my brother.
And for Gretchen: the most wonderful daughter
a father could ever be given.

FOREWORD

This is a story about God.
It is a narrative of witness.
A chronicle of wonder.

The journey spans over a half century and includes a memorable cast of characters who are real. But my story is primarily about God—what He does for us, what He does within us and finally, what He does *through* us.

End of sentence.

Unfortunately, because of the way things are done in the world, I've had to put all this down in something we call a book, though I wish it were otherwise. You see, instead of your having to *read* it, I'd much rather *tell* it to you just as people once told stories around camp fires for thousands of years, well before anyone came up with the idea or means of writing them down. For that reason, as I wrote it, I kept seeing the two of us having an extended conversation in your living room or study, across the kitchen table, sitting on the deck, or under a shade tree or wherever your favorite listening place is. And as you hear my story, I hope you will become attuned to the rhythm and cadence of my voice, for that should bring us closer together than the printed page ever can.

Who should read it?

Christians, Jews, agnostics, atheists—whatever, whomever. Your denomination, faith (or lack of one) doesn't enter into the equation. Same goes for your age, education, career or calling. My message begs to be heard by an audience whose dimensions defy normal boundaries. Moreover, without your even being aware of it, at some point in the process, you may discover that part of your story is merging with part of mine. So much the better. A special note: if you're a parent of a child soon to be a teenager or one who already is, make sure you read it this weekend. If you're a single parent along with this, plus making your way in business, start reading it tonight. Or if you're someone whose faith has been lukewarm, but you've been yearning to know God with a closeness and certainty–a God who can rejoice with you, weep with you, hurt with you, bleed with you–then start reading it the minute you get home. Just tell the world to take the rest of the day off.

Who or what, can you expect to meet in its pages?

First of all, you will get to know a few angels—up close. However, I do *not* mean little girls with golden wings who come out onto the stage in the church's nativity drama. When I say angels, I mean just that: real, live *angels*. There is a disturbing irony in the fact that most of us read the accounts of angels in the Old and New Testaments, and we smile contentedly and say to ourselves, "that's nice" then catch the bad news at six and eleven. Whoa, pardner. Hold it right there. If people were visited by angels way back then, it can still happen now. Conversely, if it does *not* happen now, then we must seriously entertain the possibility that it did not happen *then* either and that the whole thing is just one big myth. Except I know it isn't. I didn't but I do now, and that's why I've had to tell this story. If you find yourself wondering when they will appear, be patient. They will show up at the precise moment of need. Someone far wiser than I once remarked that God is slower than molasses but always on time.

In my story, you will meet the living God, and you will find He is not a seasonal God. He is not something or someone who comes and goes. He is not a Being that we book for a four-week engagement, then hold Him over if the audience likes Him, to be brought back next year with an all-new show and cast of thousands. God is for all time and until the end of time, and then gloriously revealed to believers and unbelievers alike.

xii

Who else will you meet?

Well, on the flip side of the coin you will get to meet The Enemy. If this brings a puzzled frown to your face, let me spell it out for you: S-A-T-A-N. No horns. No hooves. No tail. No fire coming out of his mouth or fiendish laughter. This is no camped up Hollywood caricature. To the contrary, The Enemy comes calling in the most ordinary garb. He could be an insurance salesman, the guy who delivers bread to the supermarket, sorts mail in the post office, a soldier, a CEO, a senator—whatever. And, to be perfectly politically correct, the *he* could be a *she*.

Why have I written it?

Certainly not to get rich. Publishing seldom works that way for unknown writers, least of all those writing about their relationship with God. If you doubt this, then the next time you're at a dinner party, try switching the conversation to earnest talk about God. Instantly, a deathly pall will come over the table, a throat or two will be cleared, and someone will break the silence by saying, "Betty, this souffle is wonderful. You must give me the recipe."

Nor did I have in mind anything as insane as running for public office or attempting to boost my standing in the United Methodist Church. (I don't have one.) I have written it because I believe the importance of what God has done through me offers meaning and relevance and perhaps redemption for many people whose names I may never know. It is my hope that the hearing of my story may bring you—or someone you give the book to— out of bondage wherein one has been acting out the dual roles of both warden and prisoner. Of course, only those who have lived in handcuffs know how sweet it is to have them taken off one's wrists.

At times, my story has the grain and feel of rough sawn lumber; indeed, you may well pick up a splinter in the hearing. It is painfully personal, for I have not ducked the hard and disturbing issues of the life I once lived outside the Kingdom. But lest we forget, the Old Testament itself is hardly all milk and honey. I have tried to stick with what a generation ago, we used to call the straight skinny.

Now at this point, you may be thinking: oh, good: this book is going to explain who God is. Heaven forbid. (He has, in fact, done just that.) I am not after an *explanation* of God—or a formula or theory that will neatly lay out all the pieces of a theological argument so that when you finish reading it, you can say, "ah, hah—now I've got it. God is this. Or God is that. Or God is this plus that. Or this *minus* that. Or any of a number of equally ludicrous and endless combinations. The fact is: the most brilliantly conceived hypothesis or carefully constructed theory will always leave gaping holes through which something that was not intended at all will either crawl into or leak out of, depending upon how you look at things. And the way I look at things—if we reduce God to an explanation, as all too many people want to do these days—then we have to settle for praying and sharing our deepest secrets with an *Almighty Explanation* or *Gracious Formula* or *Heavenly Equation*. You can quickly see where this is leading us.

This is a firsthand, real-time, real-world verifiable account of how God works *through* us. Not theoretical, not theological. Not some old, musty lecture covered with a patina of chalk dust. Nor a slickly packaged proposition offered up from the lectern for debate, from there to be handed over to a study committee until the millennium. As I said, I'm not talking about things that took place two thousand years ago, but rather in the last half century, and I have told it in language that does not require a college degree, a thesaurus or a Bible dictionary to get through it. It is not festooned with verses or numerous references to Scripture as though I were trying to add credence to what the Lord has done in my life. God does not need footnotes. His works and words speak for themselves and do so in a voice that is older than time and more authentic than anything the pedagogues might scratch out on the blackboard.

The events are real. The dates are real. The people are real, and in most cases, I have used their real names as well. More than a few of the events I describe might more aptly be called miracles—scaled down variants of loaves and fishes—but you'll have to decide that for yourself. Again, I urge you to focus on one thesis throughout: this is God's story, not mine. I serve only as a player: an extra written into the script at the right time and place. An instrument through which He has worked His will. What kind of instrument, you ask? What about a tuning fork? When it picks up vibrations, it sends these back out to be received by others and sets an amazing cycle in motion. Of course, if you stand back from a tuning fork and observe, it appears that very little is actually taking place. However, if you put your ear close and listen, you will hear the thrumming of the earth, the energy of the Kingdom resonating through you or me on its way to God knows where or God knows who. I am such an instrument. We all are, if we are open to receiving His message.

One caveat: If some of the things you hear in my story dismay, disturb or shock you, please remember that you are listening to the person I *once* was—which is to say, someone who knew no more about God than a hog does about Sunday. God was an interesting and diversionary hobby. When it suited my purposes to bring Him into a conversation or relationship, I did so much as a magician pulls a rabbit out of a hat, though ultimately it was *He* who returned the favor by snatching me out of hell.

For the record, I was born a Jew, the third son of a Russian immigrant. Growing up Jewish in the south in my childhood was no picnic, and as I retell the stories of what our world was like back then, I realize they may sound like fables, but read, then decide. I've had to put it all down in print because wherever I go now, people ask me what happened. *How* did it happen? What does it mean to you? And they want to hear all this over a cup of coffee because "they only have ten minutes to spare." Unfortunately, life doesn't work that way, and we both know it.

From the standpoint of my faith, I subscribe to the same beliefs held by early Jewish Christians in the first century, and no, I am not one of the group who call themselves Jews for Jesus. No offense: in fact, I find their ardor rather refreshing. However, I prefer to think of myself simply as a Jewish Christian. What really matters is that when a Jew meets up with the gospel, it's always an 8.5 on the Richter. That's the "big one" that will shake us out of our socks and right down to our souls.

Finally: it is my sole purpose that upon hearing my story in full, you may find yourself moved toward confronting the fact of a living God and the Son of God and Son of Man—Jesus Christ. The Messiah.

That is my prayer. By the way, in case you're interested, it should take the average reader no more than two hours to accompany me on this journey and in the process hear my story. On the other hand, to graft my story onto *your* story, then begin to *live* it, might well take the rest of your life. Bottom line on all this?

God lives.

God listens.

God loves.

Everything else is up for grabs.

Now let's get this show on the road. . . .

Rewind the tape . . .

Glassboro, New Jersey. It is the afternoon of November 10, 1938. Trees display their bare limbs under a sullen sky while a fitful wind whips at leaves raked into small piles in the gutters of University Boulevard. There is an unseasonable chill in the air, and townspeople remark to one another that it's never gotten this cold so early, and they turn up the collars of their coats.

The previous night had witnessed the atrocity called *Kristal Nacht* in Nazi Germany. Thousands of Jews had their little shops wrecked and burned and had then been brutalized, some even murdered. Little did the world know this was an ominous portent of what would come to be known as the Holocaust.

In any event, this particular afternoon found me and my brother Dick home from school and waiting for Mother to serve up cocoa and cookies. Suddenly, we heard shouts outside, then the sound of what appeared to be hail. We walked out onto the front porch to find a group of eight or ten boys riding their bicycles in a circle in the street while throwing rocks at our house and shouting, *Verdamnte Juden*, the translation of which I will spare you. Some were wearing the Brown Shirts of the Hitler Youth movement complete with swastika arm bands.

Mother shouted at them to stop, but seeing this had no effect, herded us inside and called the police who begrudgingly came and gave the boys a slap on the wrist for what they described as a harmless prank. However, for me, it was my first look at the face of evil. I have carried that recollection vividly in my mind to this day.

I was six years old.

CHAPTER 1

Minerva - mother
Meyer - father

Exodus.

I was <u>born in Philadelphia</u> when it was still the city of brotherly love. (Weren't they all, back then?) It had been my mother's home and her parents' adopted home since Max Finzimer, a German Jew, had come to America to start a candy factory in the late nineteenth century. My mother, Minerva, was one of eight girls born to Max and Hannah. My <u>father, Meyer,</u> was a shy boy, who with his brothers and their parents, <u>had left Russia to escape the onslaught of</u> the *pogroms.* For Russian Jews, that was like a hog killin', with their being the livestock.

Minerva and Meyer met in the <u>eighth grade,</u> he with his baggy pants held up by a piece of string and she with her coy smile and auburn curls. They were <u>married a</u> heartbeat <u>after high school,</u> and Daddy went to work for United Fruit as a buyer of bananas in the Caribbean: flying around the islands on puddle-jumper planes landing on dirt airstrips, riding narrow gauge railways that snaked through the jungles to the banana plantations then sometimes hitching a ride back on the steamers, the banana boats that brought the fruit to the northern markets. He brought the same talents to bear while working for his brothers who were the largest importer of bananas in Philadephia, but Daddy always wanted to be his own man and left the family business just about the time the depression hit. He started pounding the sidewalks selling stationery door to door for ten cents a box. That's when Mother cut soles for his shoes out of cardboard. Then, in the mid-thirties, he went on the road selling bushel baskets for a company headquartered in New Jersey but whose main manufacturing plant lay on the banks of the Roanoke

River in a small town in eastern North Carolina.

In 1940, a great spring flood inundated the plant, and the northern owners decided to sell out to a trio of local buyers. Daddy had a decision to make. He could stay with the former owners whose generosity left something to be desired, or he could come south as part of the deal and go to work for Jesse Whitley, N.C. Green and George Harrison, true southern gentlemen to the man. That, as we like to say today, was a no brainer for Meyer. Thus did the Levin family wind up in Williamston, a town that lay simmering on the edge of the Great Dismal Swamp in a land where tobacco was king and peanuts stood next in line.

Meyer, Minerva, Robert, Richard and Ronnie—we three boys being referred to by Mom as the Three R's. If it sounds like a vaudeville touring troupe, in a way I suppose, we were. We had a last name no one pronounced right, a heritage no one cared about, a religion no one wanted to hear about and an accent people laughed at. Worst of all, we were broke. Overnight, we had gone from a culture of bagels to one of beagles, exchanging a steam heated brick row house in Philadelphia in shouting distance of a kosher deli for a nine-hundred-square-foot clapboard dwelling on a dirt road with two wood stoves and a resident mouse in the kitchen.

At its best, southern hospitality in Williamston was like a magnolia blossom on a June night, its heady fragrance almost overpowering. But along with it, there was another kind of scent, this one not nearly so fragrant. More like the stench of something rotting out there on the edge of the swamp: a rank, ugly presence. We didn't know it, but the Ku Klux Klan was alive and well, having lynched two black men only a year before, leaving them hanging on a tree in the swamp.

The next summer was 1941, and we moved into a duplex for sixteen dollars a month that featured an honest-to-goodness oil stove. No more chopping wood. The Levin's were coming up in the world, and we boys were also about to come of age as entrepreneurs, though we wouldn't have recognized the word. All we *did* know was that one June morning just before dawn, our mother woke us up, told us "the truck was in," and that was our introduction to the peach business.

Let me explain . . . you see, in the summer, Daddy made selling trips to that part of the Carolina's called the peach belt—from Candor and Ellerbe and eventually down into Spartanburg County in South Carolina. One day, while in the packing shed, he noticed that though the best fruit—U.S. No. 1 Grade A—was being packed and loaded for shipment up north, other smaller trucks were being loaded out back, in which the peaches were just dumped up loose. Daddy asked the owner about this, and the man said, "Meyer, those are culls. We get fifty cents for 'em. I look at it as found money. Otherwise, we'd have to let them sit there until they went soft, and then we'd have to haul 'em to the dump."

Daddy drove back home, turning it over in his mind the whole way. The next day, he had a truck rolling to the owner with a load of baskets, and he called him.

"Lindsay, my truck is due in this afternoon. I put 100 empty baskets on there—stuff we would throw out. How about filling those up with culls for my boys. I'm gonna take a chance on it, and if I lose, I lose. By the way, what are you gonna charge me?"

"For your boys, Meyer? Shoot, how about a quarter?"

The deal was done.

And that's how and why at four in the morning, Mother came into the bedroom and said, "Boys, you have to get up now. The truck's in."

It was the last week in June. School was out, and summers in that part of the world were long, hot and steamy. We didn't have anything to do anyway, so we figured this might turn out to be fun. Well, very quickly we came to the conclusion that grading peaches under a single light bulb, picking out the slops and slapping at mosquitoes while shooing away gnats was not fun. Dick had built the grader all by himself, and I guess it was what you would call low tech or maybe *no tech*. Basically, it was a six foot long wooden incline wide at the top end and narrow at the bottom. Bob would pour the peaches in at the top, they would tumble down toward my end, I'd pick out the slops and stuff that was just too bad, and Dick would top off the baskets and arrange

3

them in a neat stack. My brothers staked out an area in downtown Williamston right between the big tobacco warehouses where five streets came together. It was used for parking when the market was on. Otherwise, being city property and just dirt, no one paid much attention to it.

Saturday morning came, and the country folk came into town as they always did, to do their shopping. We made a big semi-circular display of baskets, tilting them up so that people driving by could see them, and we were in business. That night, we came home dead tired, sweaty, our faces red from having been in the sun all day, and Daddy was there to greet us. "What'd you do with the peaches? You didn't leave them there, did you?"

"No sir," said Bob, flashing that big wide grin of his. "We sold 'em."

"All of them?" Daddy was incredulous.

They nodded. My two brothers unloaded their pockets and gave him all the money. There were worn crinkled bills, mostly ones, a few fives, and with Daddy's help, we counted it out on the kitchen table.

"Jumping Jehosaphat. There's almost $200 here. You sold 'em for that much—two dollars a bushel?" Mother said, "Daddy, keep your voice down, and you boys clean up for supper."

"Yes ma'am," we said, as one voice. Dick said, "We had to keep on grading out the softs, that's why it didn't come out exactly even." "And Daddy," I piped up, "we even sold the softs for a dollar. People wanted to make ice cream out of them."

I realize now that Daddy was struck dumb by the fact that three boys had made more in one day than most people made in a month. Mother, proud of us as always, fed us a good supper. After dinner, we took our baths, scrubbed off the grime—she made sure of that—then came into the living room to cool off by sitting in front of a small electric fan. Daddy picked up the phone and called his friend.

"L.G., this is Meyer. I got another truck coming down Monday. This time, put on *two* hundred."

We discovered the miracle of cash flow, and look out Martin County, the Levin boys were in business! When the season

4

ended, Daddy took the money and thrilled my mother by buying a modest brick bungalow right across from the high school. Six months later, the Japanese bombed Pearl Harbor and Bob left UNC and enlisted in the Air Corps. After eighteen months of training, he was piloting a B-24 over Nazi Germany, and a star hung in our window.

The next summer and those after, Dick and I were well known around town and the county as the "peach boys." With each successive summer, we kept gaining experience and had a lot better feel for what we were doing. For instance, during the week, business was slack. Townspeople would be out and about, but farmers and their families simply were not around. And after three days of lackluster sales, we decided if they couldn't come to us, we'd go to them. When I was old enough to drive—fourteen—Daddy bought an old green Bell Telephone truck, and I would load up the truck on Monday morning for a run out in the country but soon discovered that selling during the day was no good. The man, the head of the house, was out working in the field, along with his young'uns, and there was no way he was going to stop working and come in from the field to talk about buying peaches. I learned that the best time to hit people was early in the evening. Since it stayed light until well after nine, I had a good four to five hours of selling time, but I soon discovered that Monday nights were no good. They were broke. Wednesday nights just as bad. Folks went to prayer meeting. Friday nights were the best. They left the fields a bit earlier than usual, and since this signalled the end of the work week, the family always had a big dinner and were in a good mood, excited about going to town the next morning. Plus one other important thing. They hadn't spent any of their money yet.

Now in those days, frozen foods were unknown. People "put up" peaches, along with tomatoes, okra, corn, squash, beans, beets and whatever else they grew on their farm. But peaches didn't and couldn't grow in eastern North Carolina, so long about January, when a family craved something sweet after Sunday dinner, there was nothing better than opening a Mason jar of peaches that had been sitting there under the sideboard or out in the pantry since way back in July. To buy them in the stores would take money, and besides, everybody knew that peaches you put up yourself were far better than anything you could buy in a can.

Black or white, young or old, it made no difference. Generally the drill went like this. I'd pull off the dirt road, then down another and into a yard swept clean by a straw broom, and suddenly a passel of young'uns, the boys wearing overalls, the girls, flour sack dresses, would pour out of the house and come running up to the truck, shouting, "Momma, Momma, the peach man's here." By now, of course, they knew me. You see, I had learned if I went out there on Thursday afternoon and left a sample—one big, beautiful, sweet, ripe peach with the youngest child at the house, and told her to be sure to tell her daddy that I would be back by the next night, it worked like a charm. I was received like royalty.

This worked fine for two weeks, and then one night, I had the unexpected happen. A man came out to the truck to see the peaches, but didn't buy. He told me he had bought a bushel the week before from someone else that had parked up at the crossroads near the store, but when he got them home, he discovered to his dismay that the farther down he went in the basket, the smaller the peaches got. I received this same reception at three more houses, and I realized that whoever my competition was, he was killing me.

I drove home that night and shared the news with Daddy. He was out on the back steps with his cigar. Mother didn't like them in the house. He puffed silently for a moment, then said, "Put the big ones on the bottom."

"Sir?"

"Son, it doesn't matter if people see the little ones on the top. Just as long as the farther down you go into the basket, the bigger they get, and make sure that the biggest of all are on the bottom. That's the only way these people are going to believe you."

I dumped out all the baskets and fixed them like he said, then went back out in the country, since I had two hours of selling time left. I went back to the house where I hadn't made a sale. The man

6

came out barefooted, wearing fresh overalls. His hair was still wet from his bath. He waved at me again and said, "I'll buy some of your peaches, but not if they get smaller on the way down." He smiled a crooked smile.

I said, "Here, I'll let you see for yourself. You pick the basket." He chose one from the back row. I brought it down off the truck, dumped it out into an empty basket. He looked at the peaches, looked at me, spit his tobacco, then turned to a tow-headed young'un alongside of him and said, "Boy, go tell your momma to come on out here if she wants some peaches—and be quick about it."

And that was all there was to it. One family told another, and though I didn't realize it, I was building something called "brand loyalty," and my word came to be known and respected up and down every back road in Martin County. My competitor came to wonder why people would not buy from him anymore but preferred to wait for that little boy in the green truck. I don't know if he ever found out my secret, but I wasn't about to tell him.

Not then. Not ever.

CHAPTER

2

Going to school was no picnic.

Tougher for me because I was a skinny little kid with glasses and couldn't swing a bat very well, catch a football or much else that seemed to matter to the other kids. I could tell jokes, though, and that helped. Then came Christmas. I had never really paid much attention to Christmas carols before, but singing them in school, I thought they were the most beautiful music I had ever heard, though I took pains not even to hum them in the presence of Mother. She was adamant on this point. Naturally, we didn't have a Christmas tree either. Upon visiting the homes of my friends during school break, I would invariably find these gigantic trees, beautifully decorated, and I would stand before them, my mouth open in wonderment. Secretly, I yearned for us to have a tree of our own, but it was not to be. Moreover, when friends came to play at our house, I had to explain that Jews did not celebrate Christmas, but something called Chanukah. Being my friends, they listened politely with a few "uh huhs," but that was about it.

If Christmas was discomfiting, Easter drew blood.

That's when the local ministers would come to school during Holy Week, a different one preaching everyday in chapel, and I can remember their florid faces shiny with sweat, growing even more red as the words came pouring out in a spray of spittle, eyes glazed, and worst of all, that threatening finger aimed right at me like the barrel of a forty-four. The drill was always the same: the Jews killed Jesus. We betrayed Him. We nailed Him up on the cross and according to these preachers, did everything vile and nasty and ugly that could ever be done to anyone. It was the

9

olympics of meanness, and we had won the gold medal. I would sit there all the while in stony silence, just knowing the preacher knew my name and was looking straight at me. There were only three or four Jewish kids in the entire assembly of three hundred, which gave a whole new meaning to the word minority. I have to smile when I hear some of my black friends say, "Well, it's different with you, Ron. People look at us and know what we are, but all white folks look alike."

Wrong.

Everyone not only in the school but in the entire community knew we were Jews and could identify us on sight as easily as if we had been wearing an arm band with a yellow star as was then the case in Nazi Germany. The thing is: I didn't even know who Jesus *was*, but that didn't seem to matter, for during Easter—in fact, anytime it pleased them—the game was always the same: let's run Ronnie home, knock him down, he's little and can't fight back. Rub his face in the dirt, put sand in his mouth and give him a bloody nose for good measure. I would finally manage to get up and run, hearing their taunts trailing after me, "Sheeny, Christ killer, godd - - - kike." Thus for me, Easter was a woefully painful time, anticipated not with joy, as those of you who are Christians experienced in your childhood, but rather with a terrible, sinking dread.

I'd arrive home from these encounters, burst into the house with tears streaming down my dirty face, shirt torn, and stomach or shins hurting from where I'd been kicked, and I would ask my mother: "Did we kill Jesus?" She would shake her head with regal authority while setting out milk and my favorite cookies. She said it was better we didn't talk about it. No matter—I would persist.

"But Mom, who *was* Jesus?" Mother explained that Jesus was a wise man, a prophet, but that we did not kill Him—the Romans did.

"But Momma, the man in chapel said that we *did*. If we didn't do it, then why does he say it? He said that Jesus was the Son of God and that we killed the Son of God." She would shake her head, mutter something in Yiddish, then give me a second helping of cookies.

When I told Mother we sang hymns at chapel, she demanded that I not sing the words, but "pretend I was singing." I would stand there, listening to the words of *Onward Christian Soldiers*, a great favorite for whoever was preaching, and as I heard the voices around me swell in unison, I wondered exactly who these "soldiers" were. I didn't get it. Weren't there Jewish soldiers in the army as well. My brother was bombing the Nazis, and *he* was a Jew. So how come we didn't sing, *Onward Jewish Soldiers*, too?

As far as keeping our traditions alive, my mother did what every good Jewish mother should. Every Friday night, she would light the *Shabbas* candles and say the prayer with us. Then twice a year, for *Rosh Hashanah* and *Yom Kippur,* we would pile in the car and drive 48 miles to Rocky Mount, where along with other Jewish families from eastern Carolina, we would gather to worship on the top floor of the Masonic Temple. The service was orthodox, or so close to it no one knew the difference, and conducted almost entirely in Hebrew. Most of us kids could barely understand a word, and when you add to that a rapid fire delivery from those reading the Torah, it was a great mystery. All we knew was that we had to sit completely motionless. If we scratched, sneezed or yawned, we received a blistering look not only from Mother but from every other grown-up sitting nearby. The rabbi invariably had a full beard, wore a stern, foreboding look, and for the longest while, I wondered if he were actually God and knew all the bad things that I had done. Thus I took great pains to avoid his dark, piercing eyes that I knew could see right through me.

After services were over, we would drive back through the endless miles of flat grey land, the windows down, the September air blowing on our faces like a blast furnace as acre upon acre of bare tobacco stalks sped by. These would be intermingled with fields of cotton where the pickers would look up momentarily, their eyes like bolls staring at us in white wonder out of a sea of black faces.

11

When I went back to school the next morning, I would try to explain to my friends where we had been, for all they knew was that it was some kind of Jewish holiday. Once I tried telling them it was our New Year, but with it being September and still hot, and Christmas still three months away, the thought of celebrating New Year's before cotton was even in must have seemed very strange to them.

In the winter of 1944 while the famous Battle of The Bulge was raging in Belgium, an incident occurred, the memory of which is still clearly etched in my mind. It was one of those rare days in mid-December. The wintry sun had broken through a three-day overcast, and the mercury was in the mid-sixties. Mr. David Schwartz was a clothing salesman from Philadelphia: slight, bespectacled, graying man in his mid-fifties, in town for one of his seasonal selling trips. And after having called on several of his customers, he had gone into a small cafe for lunch. The proprietor was one N.L. Gadsen, whom I knew since he was a customer on my afternoon paper route. Gadsen lived on the other side of the tracks in what we called "old town," in a weather-beaten clapboard house. He was a tall, raw-boned man in his mid-thirties who was known to have a bad temper, especially when he drank, which was most of the time. Mr. Schwartz walked inside the cafe, sat down at the counter and ordered a chicken sandwich with a glass of milk. When he had finished and went to the register to pay, Gadsen told him it was a dollar. Now that does not seem like much to us now, but in today's currency a dollar would translate into *ten* dollars, clearly an outrageous price for a sandwich and a glass of milk.

Mr. Schwartz complained, saying he thought he was being overcharged, and Gadsen said, "Listen, you kike sonofabitch, you g-dam Jews got all the money anyway, so just pay up and get your sheeny ass out of here!"

Mr. Schwartz protested again, and Gadsen came out from behind the counter, grabbed him and threw him through the screen door, the body landing on the sidewalk out in front. Then Gadsen began kicking the older man in the head, the glasses shattering, teeth and blood lying spattered all over the sidewalk,

12

and continued to do this while cursing the prostrate figure. Passersby stopped, gawked, then went on about their way. Someone called the police, they came, followed by an ambulance, and Mr. Schwartz was taken to the local hospital. He suffered a cerebral hemorrhage from the violent blows to his head and went into a coma. His family was notified. His wife was in Baltimore.

His two sons? They were fighting with the 82nd Airborne at the Battle of The Bulge, to put an end to the most evil force the world has ever known. Once the battle was over, the sons flew back to the states for emergency leave, came into town wearing forty-fives and threatened to hunt down Gadsen and kill him. There was a trial, and Gadsen received a six months suspended sentence for involuntary manslaughter. The sons loaded the coffin containing their dead father onto the train, taking him back to Baltimore. My mother was so angry she could have spit bullets. Then one afternoon, a week or so after the incident, I was delivering the *Norfolk Ledger Dispatch,* and I had made up my mind that I would not leave Gadsen a paper. As I came by his house, he was out in the yard, saw me pass without slinging a paper down the walk and shouted after me: "Hey, you little Jew bastard, where's my paper?"

I screamed back over my shoulder as I pedalled furiously. "I'm not gonna bring you one anymore." He stormed out after me, breaking into a run, but I was too fast for him. When I got home later, I told my mother what I had done, and she first looked at me, her eyes wide in fear, then gave me one of those cryptic smiles of hers along with a hug and told me to clean up for supper. After that, when I went on my route, I was always careful to give Gadsen's house a wide berth.

Somehow, Gadsen kept his cafe, grew perpetually meaner and gradually drank himself to death. I put down all these things because today, almost a half-century later, the same disease is endemic in the land.

Burn a black man soaked with gas. Burn eight million Jews in the ovens. Shoot up a mosque in Hebron. Bludgeon a white truck driver in L.A. No matter what Crayola you pick from the

13

box, the lesson to be learned is simple. Issues may be black and white or even grey. But all God's children bleed red.

And you can take that to the morgue.

CHAPTER
3

The summer of 1945 came, we sold peaches as usual, then in August, they dropped "the bombs" and the war was over. Dick was entering the eleventh grade, and it had been decided that in order to be properly prepared for college, he would attend Oak Ridge, a military school near Greensboro. As usual, Daddy was on the road calling on farmers from Upstate New York all the way to Florida, selling baskets, telling stories and jokes, making friends, meeting people and having what I now understand must have been a wonderful adventure.

For the Levin family, Sunday mornings were strangely empty. We didn't go to Sunday School or church or any of the other functions that took place on that special day. We could hear the church bells ringing from all over town, and somehow that only made us feel more isolated. Then one day Mother announced she had an idea. Actually, if it came from Mother, it was a commandment set in stone to rival the tablets Moses brought down from Mount Sinai. Mother had come to the conclusion that it was time I learned more of our Jewish heritage, so she had bought a set of three books, *The History of the Jewish People*. I started to read these on my own, but it was determined that I would benefit more from a course of organized study. There was only one person qualified to teach me, and his name was Sid Zimmerman. Mr. Zimmerman owned a tiny ladies' clothing store on Main Street where he lived in the back with his wife, Rose, and son, Joey. Every Sunday, then, while our Christian friends were having Sunday School, I rode my bike downtown, parked it in the alley behind the store and went in for Sunday school, Jewish style. The Zimmerman's lived in an area the size

15

of a living room, and that included kitchen, bath—everything. I would find Mr. Zimmerman in his tattered bathrobe, unshaven, and while sipping from a glass of hot tea, he would walk Joey and me through the wonderful Old Testament stories. This went on for a while, and then either I quit coming or Mr. Zimmerman grew tired of the sessions—I'm not sure which.

Sid Zimmerman was what in those days people called "a character." A small, slim man, he had a cocky manner about him, in the way he spoke and walked, this accentuated by a perpetual mocking grin on his face. With his flashy clothes and sporting ways, he seemed more like a vaudeville comedian than he did a businessman. He had grown up in Baltimore where he had become the leading pool shark in the city, and once he had even considered becoming a rabbi. Instead, he had taken "a line of clothes" on the road, and traveling through Williamston in the late thirties decided this was a good place to start a business. He rented a little storefront for eight dollars a month, moved his new family in the back that boasted one grimy window looking out on an alley. He hung out a sign on the front, and that was it. Interestingly enough, this was a pattern repeated again and again in the south by peddlers who would come through town with a pack on their backs and decide to put down roots. History records that more than one large department store chain was started in just that fashion.

Directly across the street from Zimmerman's was the town's leading men's and ladies' clothing store owned by two Jewish brothers, the Lifson's: Cy and Isadore. In contrast to Sid, they were quite prosperous, dressed in three-button suits, smoked cigars and wore big gold rings. Lifson Brothers was the place where the best families in town shopped for all their clothes, while just across the street, right in their face, was Zimmerman's Ladies' Ready-To-Wear. The Lifson's looked down on Sid Zimmerman because he made his family live in the back of the store, and Sid told jokes, he laughed too loud, and for crying out loud, the *schlemiel* didn't even own a car. They were embarrassed by him. Sid shrugged all this off and in response, regarded them with thinly-veiled contempt. It was a mild, low level

16

running feud, and something that the whole town knew about. Small town intelligence networks operate almost at the speed of light, and Williamston was no different. If Myrtle Barnes sneezed, minutes later the whole town would know that she was coming down with a cold.

Sid took great delight in teasing what he called "the local yokels," and he would sit in front of the police station at night, swapping stories and matching wits with a group of regulars who always gathered there. When they would make fun of his being a Jew—though none of them had the foggiest notion of what that meant—Sid would fire a broadside that would rock them back on their cane chairs. One summer night, after filling my bicycle basket with books from the town library, I sneaked down the alley to stand just outside the circle of light. I heard Sid's unmistakable mocking laugh, and then someone said, "Well, hell, Sid, if you Jews are so damn smart, then why are you living in the back of that store with your wife and kid. Hell, boy, you ain't no bettern' a damn nigger."

Sid exploded. "You can say whatever you want, but my people were worshiping one God when your people were still living in trees chunking rocks at one another." He got up, letting his chair fall over and stormed off into the summer darkness, several taunts following him. I was so intent in the proceedings that I lost my balance and fell off my bike, the basket top heavy from the books. Charlie Morgan, the night policeman, heard the noise and dashed up the alley to see who was there.

"Hey, looka here, y'all," said Morgan. "I done caught me a little Jew boy spyin' on us." I shook in fear and tried to explain that I had just come to check out some books. He laughed derisively and said, "Hell, go on home to your momma, boy, but you better watch out, or I'm gonna cut those off and feed 'em to the hogs. We know how to take care of you Jew boys." As he said this, he grabbed his crotch, and the rest of the crowd roared with laughter. I leapt on my bike and pedaled home furiously down the dark streets, trying to outrun the shadows cast by the street lights. All the while I wondered what he had meant, and why people didn't like us just because we were Jewish.

17

With my father, however, it was completely different. Everyone in the entire county knew that Meyer Levin was Jewish, and he did not try to "pass" or hide it, nor did he wear it on his sleeve. His language, mannerisms and everything else about him became so much a part of the world of eastern North Carolina that you would have never known this man had been born a Russian Jew; and nearly everyone embraced him as one of their own. Certainly, this was true for what we then called the colored people, as well as the poor whites, both of whom regarded Daddy as their "boss" at the basket factory, though he was really just the sales manager. Regarding black folk, Daddy was the only buffer between them and the police, most of whom were Klan members or else in cahoots with them. When the black men who worked for my father would get into trouble on Saturday nights, their wives or girlfriends—we weren't ever sure which—would come around to the back door, and I can still hear their voices, the words pouring out in a panic-stricken rush.

"Mistuh Levin's . . . uh-ruh . . . I hates to bother you it being so late and all, but see, my man Horace, he done gone and broke bad and got hisself in a lotta trouble drinking and such, but he ain't no bad man, Mister Levin's. Lord knows he ain't. He jes— you know, a man gets to drinking and carryin' on and such, and then 'fo you know it, the po-leese come down there, and by then, he be so drunk and all, it'd be too late to do anything about it."

Against Mother's protests, Daddy would go down to the jail and make bail, and this won him the name of the "black man's Jesus." I'm sure that did not further endear us to the white townsfolk, yet, in spite of that, people were starting to warm up to the Levin family.

Now, Mother was cut from a different piece of cloth than Daddy. She had grown up under a harsh, stern father whose temper could and did explode without warning. Partially as a result of this, she approached life each morning as though she were going into battle wherein victory was determined by who was right—who was correct. Everything had to be in its place, lists were made and checked off with drill sergeant precision. When we would pile into the car and accompany Daddy on one

18

of his selling trips, we would eat at whatever place looked halfway decent, and Mother would straightaway make for the ladies' room, then come back and give us a report. She might have been a health inspector for all the restaurant owner knew. When the check was presented, Mother would go over it very carefully, and sometimes discover an error in the addition. I can remember one time it was only three cents. Daddy would protest, but Mother would say, "I don't care, it's not the money, it's the principle of the thing."

Actually, it was both, but I didn't know this then. Mom would have done the same thing if it had been a penny, for she took great pride in being right, and by her finding an error in what someone else did, perhaps that made her more nearly perfect in an imperfect world. It was her suit of armor, the only suit she could find that fit, and it gave her protection in an alien land. We boys grew up bathed in the blinding light of that ethos, and without our ever realizing it, we were gradually yet irrevocably shaped into Minerva's mold. Yet on the plus side of the ledger, this was the driving force behind her remarkable industry, perseverance, and organizational skills—gifts that ultimately won her the admiration of many, and eventually, their love. The word among the ladies of the town was that if you wanted a job done and done right, let Minerva do it.

Getting back to those restaurants I mentioned: when the waitress brought the check, Daddy paid no attention to the total— though he had the uncanny knack of adding five columns of figures, five numbers wide, in his head. Instead, he would ask for a piece of paper, then write on it words to the effect that "Mildred is the world's greatest waitress." Now, ordinarily, this wouldn't have meant very much, but my father happened to be a master craftsman of Spencerian penmanship, and he shaped his letters like Pavarotti sings, thus the note was an instant work of art. Bank presidents to truck drivers, waitresses to socialites, college professors to clerks—when receiving one of these notes from Meyer Levin, the recipients would gaze open-mouthed at the handwriting. Women would blush and men would stammer. Some people were so proud to receive such a note, they would have it framed and displayed in their office or home with pride.

Stories and jokes? My father was the county fair, blue ribbon winner. If on a Saturday morning, Meyer Levin, fresh from being on the road, showed up at the barber shop for a shave from Pete (the volunteer fire chief) the word spread and all gathered to hear his latest crop of new tales. In short, Daddy was an instant hit wherever he went. A rework of that old advertising slogan for Sara Lee: *Nobody doesn't like Meyer Levin.*

One time my father and I had gone out in the country to visit a farmer, and I remember the man taking off his straw hat, wiping the inside of the band, then putting it back on and biting off a fresh plug of tobacco.

"You know something, Mister Levin, I'll be honest with you. I was just telling somebody about you the other day, and they wanted to know how I got along with you cuz of, you know . . . you being a Jew and all that, and I told him . . . I said, Mr. Levin weren't like no other Jew I ever knowed before in my whole life."

With that, the man clapped my father on the back and shook his hand. Now to someone more stiff-necked than Daddy, that may have sounded like the classic backhanded compliment, said from ignorance and carrying the taint of bigotry, but my father saw it differently because of how God made him. He would not have recognized the words pluralism or multi-cultural. He had not attended any sensitivity workshops. He did not know what inclusivity was and would have laughed at the notion of political correctness. What he *did* have, however, was a deep, abiding humility, a love of all people and the common touch. And that's why the words of that farmer wrapped around his heart like spun gold.

20

CHAPTER

4

It was 1948, and I was headed for the eleventh grade. Satchel Paige started to pitch for the Cleveland Indians, and "Give 'em hell," Harry Truman was whistle-stopping and destined to upset Dewey in November. Israel had been rejected for membership by the UN, and "All I Want for Christmas Is My Two Front Teeth" would hit the top of the charts that fall.

In September, I went to Oak Ridge, as Dick had before me, and my first year as a "rat" was probably no less painful for me than it had been for him. Bending over a bunk and getting your butt beat with a broom was standard operating procedure for everyone, and whether one was Jewish or not had little to do with it. Unfortunately, there were the usual number of cadets who, for reasons unknown to me, disliked Jews, and it was my bad luck to be rooming on a floor where there were several of these. As a result, the beatings I received from them were delivered with an added measure of undisguised glee on their part. "Hey Abie, bend over and grab the bottom rail" became a kind of ritual that I knew was coming on a nightly basis, but I learned to grit my teeth to hold back the tears. More than once during those first several months, the thought occurred to me to leave school and go home. But my resolve to stick it out was stronger.

In any event, I was determined to be a good student, applied myself with diligence, and suddenly the school year was over. The down side was that I came home with a severe fungus infection in my feet, and my mother made an appointment for me with a specialist at Duke Hospital. One morning in June, I drove up to Durham to see him, and on the way back, just outside the town of Spring Hope, my last recollection was that the sun was very warm on my face and then as I rounded a curve, I kept hearing some kind of recurring noise from behind me.

The next thing I knew, I was sitting behind the wheel with the engine poking into the front seat, the Ford sitting in a wheat field about a hundred yards off the road, the hood up at a rakish angle, steam hissing from the radiator and little spurts of flame coming out of the carburetor. For some reason, the first thing I noticed was the large glass bottle of medicine lying on the seat beside me unbroken—right where I had placed it when I got into the car a half hour ago. I couldn't understand that, but I was too stunned to pay much attention. Then I glanced over my shoulder and saw two men coming toward me from the highway back up the hill, running through the wheat until they reached me.

"C'mon, son," said the man in the worn overalls and the sweat stained shirt. "We gotta get you out of this car." The other man was a highway patrolman. The farmer looked at the car—remember, this was a generation before seatbelts—and I remember his words. "Boy, do you go to church?" Mother had always taught us that when anyone asked us that, just say *yes* in order to avoid getting into a discussion that might turn into an argument. I nodded and mumbled "yes."

"Well, you sure God better get down on your knees this Sunday and thank the Lord Jesus for giving you your life. If I wasn't seeing this with my own eyes, I wouldn't believe it. That there Ford is a wreck, and it's only by the grace of God you're alive. Shoot fire, you ain't even got a scratch." I was going to tell him that God had nothing to do with it, but then remembering where I was, thought better of it and remained silent.

As I stood there, shaking, the patrolman said, "Can you walk?" I took a few tentative steps, and told him I was okay. Then I walked back to the car, reached in and got the bottle of medicine. The two men just stared at me and the unbroken bottle and looked back at the front half of the car that was a total wreck. As we walked up the hill, that's when I saw that the pole carrying the power lines had been broken off, lying there snapped in two like a giant matchstick. Huge blue sparks were coming out of the wires and would arc out in a crackling sound and cause small fires

22

to spring up.

Once back at the patrolman's car, he explained that he had been parked on the side of the road and had watched me pass, the car weaving erratically. He deduced because of my age and the time of day, I was not drinking, but simply falling asleep. Realizing this, he had pulled out to follow me and was blowing his horn trying to alert me, when a huge truck came barreling around the curve and would have hit me dead on had my car not left the road at that precise instant. He said that when I dozed off, my foot must have gone down on the gas pedal, because I was doing about sixty-five when I hit the pole. He said he couldn't figure out how I avoided being injured, let alone killed, and that when he'd turn in the accident report, no one would believe I got out without a scratch. When the car was finally towed back to Williamston, people looked at it and just shook their heads. I told people I was lucky, that's all. Just plain lucky. And that was that. I remembered what the farmer said about "grace," asked Mom what that meant, but she passed it off with a smile and a hug, so I forgot about it.

At the beginning of my second year, as one of two Jewish students at Oak Ridge, I was invited to attend Rosh Hashanah services in Greensboro as a guest of the famous Cone family of Cone Mills. I caught a bus into town, and a limousine picked me up at the bus station and drove me out to a mansion that was a scaled down version of the Biltmore House. He and his family were quite gracious to me, and the next morning, though I tried to be attentive during services, the responsive reading droned on, no one smiling or even looking happy. I wanted to feel good about being in a temple. I wanted to be *excited* about God, but there was always this feeling that one had to be very serious. I have since come to learn that in all too many houses of worship— especially the main line denominations—this same kind of rigidity exists, where it is not considered at all proper to express joy.

I kept envisioning God as being very angry with us and disappointed, and that if we didn't measure up, eventually He would exact his vengeance and there would be retribution. That

23

kind of God frightened me; moreover, the longer I thought about it, the more the separation grew between us. I need not have worried on this score since with the beginning of my second year at military school, there was little time for God, for now that I was a senior—a "cat"—school became great fun. I had a lot of friends, was made sergeant, and at some point during the year, and to my great surprise, was elected president of my senior class along with being made valedictorian. The latter pleased my parents greatly, but being elected president by my peers was an act of liberation. It meant people liked me and respected me, and my being Jewish had nothing to do with it. Being a Jew was something I was now starting to be proud of and feel good about, but I was a Jew only in the cultural sense. As far as "practicing" my religion or knowing God, He seemed more distant than ever.

Early that spring, I received a demerit for dust found during an inspection and as punishment was assigned to help the janitor sweep up the chapel. While I was doing one side, he sat down at an ancient upright piano and began to bang out what we then called boogie-woogie. I went over and watched, half in a trance. I told him I wanted to learn how to do that. He asked if I played at all, and I told him I had taken lessons for two years when I had been ten. Then he made me sit down and putting his big, black hands over mine, he showed me the notes and the rhythm, base line and the melody, and then how it all fit together. I made sure I got a few more demerits, just enough to be able to be sent up to help him, and by the end of the school year, I was finding my way around the keyboard with ease.

Fall of 1950 found me enrolled at UNC at Chapel Hill as a freshman. The North Korean army had overrun the South and war was on. But we freshmen paid little attention to all this, being caught up in the exhilarating freedom of being on our own for the first time. I discovered this thing called drinking and learned two things: one, it could make you very happy and two, it could make you very sick. Substance abuse was as much a part of college as going to classes, and apparently not very much has changed in the last half-century. Though the selection has widened, from what I can determine, booze is still the substance of choice. I did a little partying, but being premed and wanting to make good grades, my days and nights were filled with classes and studying. I spent time with the piano, too, learning to play and sing all the hit tunes. Plus, in a fraternity, one learns songs of a different kind, and though the lyrics were unusual, if at times, obscene, the chords were simple, and soon I became the resident pianist and entertainer at all our parties.

During Thanksgiving of my sophomore year, I came home for the holiday and on Friday night, borrowed the car and drove out to a late night spot that stayed open until the wee hours. I had heard they had a piano, and within minutes, the crowd had gathered around me, singing and laughing, all this delighting "Eva," the woman who owned the place. I'd had a couple of beers, no more, because I never really drank that much when I was playing. (Contrary to what most people think, you can't play well with a buzz on, and when you're drunk, you can't play at all.) Eva's niece was there, too: Janice. A stunning girl about my age, and we were instantly attracted to one another. As the evening wore on, I played all that wonderful beach music you might remember from the fifties, and the joint was rockin' and rollin'. Suddenly, I realized it was midnight, and I called home and told Daddy not to worry about me. He asked where I was, I told him, adding I'd be home later, and he said that was fine.

The time sped by, the crowd really getting into it. Eva gave me a cup of coffee, I took a sip, then launched into "Sixty Minute Man," with the crowd joining in when suddenly they all stopped singing, put down their beers and drinks and were looking behind me. I spun around from the upright and there stood my father. I could see his pajama bottoms sticking out from beneath his topcoat. He looked like a man who would have given anything to be somewhere else—*anywhere*. I could feel his shame and embarrassment.

"Son, your mother wants you to come home. Now!" He started to say more, then his voice broke, and he turned and left.

For a moment there was total silence, then I excused myself and drove home. When I walked in the door, Mother was sitting in the living room, one small light on, Daddy apparently having

25

gone to bed. She wanted to know who I had been out with and what I'd been doing. I told her I hadn't really been out with anyone—just having a good time playing the piano at Eva's Place.

"Who was there?"

"Mom . . . just . . . you know. People. Eva Fuller . . . Janice Gaines and—"

"I absolutely forbid you to go to that place anymore," she said, her mouth set in a grim line, the eyes hard, unyielding.

Well, I was a college sophomore, almost nineteen, and having had a real taste of freedom, nobody was going to forbid me to do anything, least of all just playing the piano and having a couple of beers. I then made the mistake of informing mother of that, and she moved to slap me, but I grabbed her arm and held it. I said, "No, Mother. I'm nineteen years old, and you're not going to hit me anymore. No more!"

She resisted me for an instant, then burst into tears, her body trembling in the folds of her housecoat.

"Mom," I said. "What is it? Why are you so upset about my being at Eva's? I only had a couple of beers. What's wrong with my having a good time?"

She held up her palm as though to silence me, nodded as she took a deep breath, then gathered the folds of her housecoat around her and began to tell me a story. . . .

"A year or so before we moved to Williamston, 1938 or '39, a Jewish salesman from up north would come through town frequently on business trips. He was quite handsome and a good talker, had money to spend, and he would frequent the after hours joints and pick up a woman. At one such place, one woman in particular caught his eye, and the other way around, they began to dance, one thing led to another, and they wound up in the back seat of his car. She would go out with almost anyone who would pay attention to her—what in those days was called a 'loose woman.' Later, when they came back into the tavern, her clothes and hair were mussed up, he had his hands all over her, and everyone was noticing them.

26

"The man took her home to her small apartment, then went back to his room at the town's only hotel, the George Reynolds. He did not know that one of the people in the juke joint was a friend of the girl's brother and had called him and told him what he had seen. At about three on Sunday morning, four men burst into the man's room, gagged him, threw a burlap sack over his head, bound his hands and took him out to the town's cemetery near a place called Doodle Hill."

Mother took a deep breath and continued. *"It was there,"* she said, *"that they tied him to a tree, took down his pants, one man took out a knife and ... and ...."* My mother took a deep breath, searching for the right word—*"and he—"*

I finished it for her. "Castrated him? Mom, they castrated him?"

She nodded, her hands shaking as she held them in her lap. "And they just left him there, tied to the tree. The police knew all about it, but didn't do anything either."

I could barely find my voice. My wrists hurt, and I realized I had been gripping my knees in a vise. "Mother, how did you find out about this?"

"I have a good friend in town who told me. I can't tell you who it is, but she was born here, and her father was born here, and she knows everything that ever happened. She said I had to promise that I would never tell anyone, and I haven't, until now. I just wanted you to know."

"Well, what happened to them—the men who did it? I mean, weren't they arrested and sent to jail?" I thought that was the way things worked, but Mom explained that the men, being leading citizens of the community and well respected, received only a six-month suspended sentence. They were leaders of the Ku Klux Klan, everyone knew it, and no judge was about to give them a harsh sentence. Any of the townspeople who thought it was wrong were probably too frightened to speak up.

"Mom," I said, not knowing where all this was going, "I'm sorry. They did a terrible thing, but what does all this have to do with my being out there at Eva's. I still don't understand."

27

As she gave a deep sigh, her shoulders sagged, and she looked straight into my face. "Son, the woman Mr. Schwartz was with . . . ."

I finished the sentence for her. "Was Eva?"

She nodded and dabbed at her eyes, then looked up at me. "And the leader of the group, the man who actually held the knife . . . he's . . . Eva's brother." She paused, trying to find her voice. "And Janice's father."

I sat there motionless, my stomach churning. Each tick of the clock on the mantle was deafening. Then slowly, inexorably, Mother began to weep. I moved toward her and we held each other for a few minutes, and then she dried her eyes, kissed me and went to bed.

Now I knew what Charlie Morgan had meant by "We know how to take care of you Jew boys." I crawled beneath the cold covers and tried to pray, but again, God was this unapproachable, severe being that I could not get close to. I closed my eyes and told God I was sorry, but of course, I didn't mean it. I wasn't sorry at all. I was angry at Him for having allowed that to happen, and I was angry that now I couldn't go to Eva's place again and wouldn't be able to see Janice, and I was angry that people were so hateful. What did we ever do to them to deserve this? I couldn't figure it out. I wondered if God knew—or even cared. I lay there for what seemed like hours turning all this over and over in my mind, finally falling asleep sometime before dawn.

I never went to Eva's again. I *did* find out there was a tree in the cemetery known to a very few people as Jew Oak. I had a friend from high school days who knew about it from his uncle, and he took me there one evening just after dusk. While he waited in his car, I stood there quietly, wondering what it must have been like. I closed my eyes, running my fingers over the bark as though it were the scaly hide of some hideous creature. I heard a man screaming, but when I opened my eyes, there was only the growing darkness around me enveloping me like a shroud.

I never went back to that place again, and I never told anyone about this for a very long time.

CHAPTER

5

For a while at college, I tried attending services at Hillel, the Jewish student religious center. I went with an earnest desire that here among people my age and in services less formal, I could get closer to God. A God whose comforting presence I could feel beside me. I didn't want a critic, a warden or a disapproving parent. I'd had enough of that already in my life. I wanted—I don't know—I guess *brother* is the right word. Someone really close to me whom I could confide in and talk to and share my dreams, my fears and my hopes. But nothing had changed. The rabbi would read, then the congregation would read. Then the rabbi would read, the words marching like wooden soldiers across the page to a joyless chant, unvarying in its tone or rhythm.

Again, I felt there was something wrong with me, yet I knew other students felt the same way, for we would talk about it back at the fraternity house. Many of them went because they promised their parents they would go, but for the most part, after services were over, the fraternity turned into one big party of beer drinking, playing cards for money, telling dirty jokes downstairs in the rec room, or driving over to neighboring Durham to "get laid," something that would have all us freshmen wide eyed with envy and astonishment. Some upperclassman would have met a telephone operator or a waitress, and two or three would pile in the car and off they'd go. When they returned, they were all smiles, burping from too much beer and bragging of their exploits, but we never knew whether to believe them or not. I'm sure it was much the same scenario in all the other fraternities as well, but doing this after services struck me as being wrong.

The irony here is that though Friday night is the time of worship for Jews, for the rest of America, it is a time to kick back, chill out, unwind, let your hair down, have fun and celebrate. In short—the start of the weekend, and every good red-blooded American kid knows what weekends are for: they're for raising hell. It is not for nothing that *Thank God, It's Friday!* has become a kind of legendary tribal cry of busting loose.

By contrast, Sunday always bears the solemn stamp of organized religion: church bells ring, people dress up, hymns are sung, and sermons preached, this followed by Sunday dinner, just as it had been in Williamston. (It's no wonder that someone once made the comment—I think it's now the title of a book—that for Jews growing up in the South, Sunday is the loneliest day in the week. That was the one day that always made us feel so out of place in the Christian world around us.)

At UNC, I plunged into college life with a passion, trying my hand at whatever came along. Writing for *The Daily Tar Heel*, running cross country, playing in the band, and with all of this, managing to maintain an A average. The fierce desire to excel, to be the best and the brightest was the driving force within me. I wanted my parents to be proud of me and craved their approval with an insatiable hunger. All the while, it never occurred to me that I knew very little of myself and almost nothing of God.

About this time, I started playing lead trumpet in my brother's dance band and was vocalist as well. On Friday afternoons, we would jam our bodies into his station wagon and hit the road to play at fashionable girls' schools, army officer's clubs, high school gymnasiums—you name it. And the thrill of applause, the crowd's way of saying, "We love you," gave me a feeling that I very much liked. It was their way of saying, "You're okay," and I needed to hear that.

I guess we all do, don't we, though we may have to wait a long time to hear it. If it even comes at all.

After nine months of this at Chapel Hill, I was hardly prepared to spend another dull, boring summer in Williamston. By now, Daddy and Dick were well into the peach business near Spartanburg, South Carolina, having rented a packing house,

30

buying fruit from growers and shipping it up north. I tried my hand at this, working under my brother's thumb, but it was not to be. Dick and I were like oil and water, and he, being older and more responsible and dependable in business matters, had my father's ear in all things—and rightfully so. There was no way I could even come close to matching his skills and talents. He knew how to operate and fix machinery, manage people, schedule production—in short, all those vital functions that are the heart of any business. I kept on trying to show Daddy what I could do by comparison, striving to win his approval, but unfortunately, it doesn't work that way, and early on, my gifts of creativity and promotional know-how weren't important to the business, though they would become so later on. Thus, after a few weeks in what for me was a kind of torture, I had all I could take of packing peaches and decided to escape to Myrtle Beach. Daddy told me in that knowing yet gentle and loving way of his that I would be back in a week, broke, but I was determined to prove him wrong.

I wound up there with about ten dollars in my pocket, my trumpet, a change of clothes and not much else. "Peaches Corner" in Myrtle Beach is the place where Sloppy Joe's Bingo, the Pavilion and the amusement park all came together. I walked inside the bingo parlor and listened to a swarthy, heavy-set man who was calling the game. He wore a wet towel around his neck and would sip from a cup of coffee then puff on a cigarette then back to the coffee. I could tell his voice was almost gone, and after getting my foot long hot dog, asked the waitress who he was, and she looked at me as though I were from Mars.

"Who, him? Hey kid, that's Dave, you know . . . Mr. Lettner. He owns the joint." She then told me that the regular bingo caller had been fired just this morning. I ate my hot dog and sat there sipping my coffee listening to everything he said. After I knew I had his spiel down pat, I went up to him when one game was over, the players clearing their cards for the next.

"Mr. Lettner," I said. "I hear you're looking for a good bingo caller."

"Yeah, that's right. You call?"

31

"Yes sir," I said glibly.

"Where?" His eyes drilled me clean.

I stared right back at him and didn't even blink. "Lucky Jim's up at Carolina Beach and Biscayne Bingo in Miami."

He waved me quiet with his hand while gazing at me intently, his glance starting at the top of my head and working its way down to my feet.

"Okay, here, kid—take the mike. It's all yours." As I reached for it and climbed up in the chair, he said, "Hey, what's your john?"

"Sir?"

"Your john . . . your handle."

"Ronnie."

"Okay, Ronnie. See if you can build the tip." I had no idea what he was talking about, but I nodded and started to call the next game. The words came easy as I repeated what I had heard him do, then started to ad lib and expand upon it. A few funny things here and there, smiles to the grey haired ladies who were playing, a couple of favorable comments about the cute grandchildren they had with them, and we were off and running. An hour later, I had the place packed—all 127 seats filled. He came up to me and gestured for the mike.

"Okay, Ronnie, take a break. I gotta call the cover-all game, and you watch and learn. After that, they'll head out of here, and we can talk." When the game was over, the people streaming out onto the sidewalk, we both sat down in a booth in the corner, and he had Ginnie bring over two coffees.

"You're pretty good," you know.

"Thanks, Mr. Lettner."

"Don't call me that. Call me Dave." I nodded. "Now, where was that you say you called?" He peered at me over the rim of his cup, puffing furiously on the cigarette.

"Lucky J—"

"Listen, Ronnie. I know every bingo parlor from Bar Harbor to Miami Beach, and there ain't no Lucky Jim's bingo and there ain't no Biscayne Bingo either." He waited.

I swallowed hard and looked down, thinking that I had just

found and lost the only job I had a chance of getting. Then he clapped me on the shoulder.

"It's all right. You did good, but lemme tell you something. Before I came here, I was a carny, riding the roads with the shows, and there's one thing I learned and learned early. Don't ever hustle a hustler. I've scammed and rube'd with the best of them, and nobody, I mean nobody, gets anything on Dave Lettner. You catch my drift?"

"Yes sir." I swallowed again, my eyes locked onto his.

"All right, here's the deal. You call six nights, five hours a night, and I spell you when you need it. Weekends, we go to midnight. I'll give you half a yard a week and all your food is half off."

He stuck out his hand, I took it, and that was it. Of course, I had no idea what half a yard was or what building the tip meant, but I wasn't going to let *him* know that. Ginnie steered me to a seven-dollar-a-week room at Captain Clint's Sea Gull Inn, just up the street, and in spite of my excitement, I was asleep before my head hit the pillow.

CHAPTER
6

This marked the start of a brand new life for me. I began to meet people who lived on the fringe of society and were called "regulars" as opposed to the tourists or marks, and I was to learn more about life from them than I could have imagined. Lesson one was how to speak a brand new language.

A fin was five dollars. A sawbuck, or "saw" for short, was ten. A double saw — twenty. A yard was a hundred. Three large meant three thousand dollars.

The *tip* was the bingo players. *Don't blow the tip* meant don't do anything that might cause the players or the audience to leave. The *flash* was the array of gifts displayed overhead, arranged to look like Tiffany's window, but in reality, it was nothing but cheap trinkets, jewelry, housewares and personal items that were bought at salvage sales. To *spif the flash* meant to re-arrange everything so it looked like a brand new assortment of gifts. Naturally, I was eating all of this up, including Ginnie's footlong's-double-chili-hold-the-onions.

In addition to the bingo, Dave and his wife, Jo, were part owners of a place called The Bowery, just a half block away, next to the boardwalk. One Saturday afternoon, Dave asked me to go down and take his wife some change. Now, The Bowery was what you called a "bust-out joint"—red tables, sawdust on the floor, twenty five cent beer and live entertainment that was high on volume and low on refinement. Every now and then there was even a good fight just to spice things up a little. While I was there and Jo was counting out the change, I asked if I could play the piano.

"Sure, why not. Hey, Ronnie, I didn't know youse played."

Jo was a tall, rawboned, brunette, hard features, a voice like sandpaper, but a generous and warm heart. It was rumored that once or twice a summer, just to show the customers who was boss, when a drunk got ugly or insulting, she would knock him off his bar stool with one punch. I would actually get to see her do this later that season. By the way, Jo was a devout Catholic and never missed confession.

"Yeah, I kinda picked it up along the way."

"Well, how 'bout that! Hey, listen—you know 'Jezebel'"?

"Jezebel" by Frankie Laine just happened to be the number one hit of the summer, and I had worked on it until I sounded more like Frankie Laine than Frankie Laine. I went up to the piano, turned on the mike, sat down and gave it all I had. When I finished, she started applauding wildly, and a couple of people at the bar did likewise, motioning me to play some more. I got off the stand, doing a modest shucks, like it wasn't any big thing, and they shouldn't really applaud, but inside my heart was doing flip-flops.

Talent show

"Hey, Ronnie, for cryin' out loud," said Jo. "I gotta get youse into the talent contest over at the pavilion tonight. And wait'll Dave hears about this. He'll go crazy! I'll tell you what. You and me are going over right now and audition while there's still time." The emcee at the pavilion knew Jo, I auditioned, and he told us to be backstage that night at eight sharp. That evening, while Dave spelled me at the bingo, Jo, her daughter and I went over to the pavilion, and I found my way backstage and waited for the other two contestants to go on. A girl in a bright floral dress and wearing pigtails came on and tap danced, and a guy who played the guitar sang one of the current rock 'n roll hits. Then I was announced and went on. There were about three hundred people in the auditorium, and I sat down at the grand piano, adjusted the boom mike, hit the opening chords and gave them a Jezebel they would never forget. I hung onto the last note as long as I could, then did a crescendo on the keyboard and stood up with a flourish. The place went wild. I won first place, five dollars, the unending admiration of Jo, and something else that I found out about the next morning.

It happened when I came into work to help spif the flash, and Dave beckoned me over to join him at his booth. "Hey, Ronnie. Jo tells me you knocked 'em out last night. And I heard it from three other people, too. I even had my own spotters in the crowd to see if you had the stuff. So anyway, kid, here's what I want you to do."

The deal was that I would go down to The Bowery on Friday and Saturday afternoons and play for a couple of hours. The regular entertainer, Wild Bill Copper, a white-haired Englishman with a cockney accent was an old music hall entertainer from London who played the banjo and accordion. He did not come on until seven, so I wouldn't be interfering with him. I could pass the pot in the afternoon and whatever I got was mine. I was a little disappointed, thinking that Dave ought to pay me over and above the half a yard I was getting for calling. He saw the look on my face and pulled me aside.

"Hey, Ronnie, you work the tip right and you'll make a nice score for yourself. Listen to me, kid. I know what I'm talking about."

I nodded, and he went back to work. Then it dawned on me that I was in a lot of trouble. What they didn't know is that I only knew about five or six songs that were current hits which would last me all of fifteen minutes. However, I did know a lot of sing-along stuff like "Working on the Railroad," "If You Knew Suzie," "Roll Out the Barrel" and a dozen or so others. Of course, I could play just about anything on the trumpet, but you couldn't do a whole gig on just solo trumpet. In spite of this, my ace was that whatever I could hear just once, I could play and sing within minutes.

I started going down to The Bowery in the morning while the clean-up crew was there and "slugged" the jukebox to hear all the latest hits of that summer. By that weekend, I had gotten nine of them down pat, and those, plus several more that I knew would get me through a set, and if anybody requested something I didn't know, I'd give it a shot. A lot of pop tunes in those days only had a half dozen chord changes, and we musicians had a saying about a tune: "If you don't know it, man, fake it till you make it."

37

That Friday afternoon, I got there a little after three just as the servicemen started coming into town for weekend liberty. Paratroopers from the 82nd at Bragg, airmen from the local air base, marines from LeJeune and Cherry Point, sailors from Charleston—you name it. That was my audience, plus a collection of textile mill workers, a few college kids, vacationing school teachers looking for kicks and whoever else happened to wander into The Bowery with a thirst for cheap beer and a few laughs.

I started out with a couple of pop hits, a rock 'n roll hit by the Coasters, and then asked for requests. Naturally, the Marines wanted to hear the "Marine Hymn" so I played it while they sang lustily, then went straight over to their table with the pot. Dimes, quarters and a few half dollars plunked in, and before I could get back, two tables of sailors said they wanted to hear "Anchors Aweigh." I passed the pot in front of their faces, looking hungry, broke and grateful, and more coins flew in. It went this way all afternoon. I played boogie, woogie, the blues, "The Saints Go Marchin' In," "The Air Force Song," the artillery song, "Jezebel," "Harbor Lights," "Sentimental Journey" and a dozen others, all interspersed with some comedy patter and wound up with a trumpet solo of "St. James Infirmary" and a Satchmo imitation which brought down the house. By five-thirty, most of the crowd had left to take a last minute swim, then go back to their motels to shower and clean up for the evening. I took the big bucket into which I had kept emptying the little pot and went out into the alley behind The Bowery to see what I had made. When I finished rolling the coins, I counted everything again to make sure I hadn't made a mistake. There was over thirty dollars for two hours of having fun. (In today's tax free dollars, that would translate into well over a hundred.) I sat there hefting the weight of the coins in the rolls, then stuffed them into my trumpet case and went back up to the Bingo for some supper.

Dave saw me walk in. "Hey, how'd you make out?"

"Ahhh . . . I took in about a saw," I said, feeling myself flush at the lie.

"See, Ronnie, what'd I tell you! Hey, what would your father say if he knew about this, huh?" He flashed me a grin then went back to his office. I ate, then went back to my room to change and clean up in time to start calling the first game.

As the days passed, and June grew into July, then August, I kept polishing my act. I could play nearly every tune on the jukebox, knew all the lyrics and special effects and things, and I had added to my store of jokes and one-liners by picking them up from everybody I ran into who had a funny story to tell. Everybody loves to hear jokes—we hear them all the time—but the secret is to *remember* them, embellish upon the original, then tell it with the right accent and facial expressions. I could do all kinds of accents—Italian, Russian, German, Mexican, Black, Jewish—it didn't matter since this thing called Political Correctness was a generation away from being born.

Finally, Dave took me off calling bingo altogether and had me doing a half hour on to spell "the Limey" as he called Bill. The crowd starting calling for me more and more, and finally Bill demanded that it was either him or me: that he didn't like splitting the pot. Dave called his bluff, and Bill quit. I found this out when I came in the next night, and I said, "Where's Bill?"

"Who knows?" said Jo. "So anyway, this means you're it. Can you handle it, Ronnie?"

I nodded, she threw me a wink, and that was it. Talk about being thrown into the fire. When you're nineteen and facing a crowd of two-hundred beer drinking vacationers, you have to keep a tight rein on them, or things can get ugly in a hurry. I had learned when they were hungry for country or blues or rock and roll or "Happy Birthday" to their girlfriend—whatever. I also learned to tell when a fight was starting to brew, and I would get them all singing "God Bless America" which did three things: everybody would stand up, it would put them in a good mood and defuse the situation, and thirdly, I would pitch it in a higher key than usual that would strain their voices, make them thirsty so that when we finished and I would raise my beer mug and say, "Okay, you bums, bottoms up," the whole room would finish their beers and order another round. Jo thought that was miraculous and could not get over how well it worked. I'd finish the set with a medley of sing-alongs that everybody knew from memory, then take a break.

I was making so much money it was crazy. Probably the equivalent today of a thousand a week, most of it tax free; and for a nineteen year old, that was incredible. I was on the radio doing commercials, and wherever I went along the beach, the other regulars recognized me and christened me "The Bowery Kid."

That was also the summer of my introduction to sex. Now, in those days, women had a thing for musicians. I don't know how it is now. My experiences were a breathtaking journey into the mysteries and pleasures of the flesh, something that heretofore I had barely known. I had fame, fun, money and freedom from anybody bugging me to do this, do that. For a nineteen-year-old kid, what more could life possibly offer?

Then, one Saturday night in August, as I was pounding out "Down Yonder" for the redneck crowd, Jo caught my eye from behind the bar and gestured with her head. I gazed through the dimly lit, smoky interior but couldn't see what she was pointing at. I went back to playing, glancing up at her, and again, she gave me the high sign. The joint was packed: standing room only and as my eyes roved over the room once more, I saw them sitting way back in the corner.

Mom and Dad.

I kept on playing without acknowledging that I saw them. Then at break, I turned on the jukebox, the music went up, the crowd began to empty out, and I went over to see my folks. After the usual hugs and handshakes, I sat down, and then Jo came over to join us.

"What'd I tell you, Mizzus Levin," she said. "It's a nice joint, ain't it, and we run a clean operation. Hey, Ronnie," she said, turning to me, "your mom and dad called up at the Bingo and wanted to know what time youse went on and all, so I reserved this special table for them. They wanted to surprise you."

"Well," my father said. "This is . . . this is really nice, Mrs. Lettner."

Jo said, "Yeah, Mr. Levin, it's somethin', ain't it!"

My mother sat there in stony silence, sipping a coke. Here was her son, a nice Jewish boy, soon to be Phi Beta Kappa, premed student, valedictorian, playing piano in a beer joint, and worse yet, up here on a stage in the infamous Bowery where all the people from Williamston would see me and come back and *tell* her they had seen me. That much I hadn't realized until Daddy told me much later. Mother was embarrassed beyond belief.

"I hope you're not running around all night and—" My mother let the rest of the sentence trail off.

"Oh, Mizzuz Levin, don't you worry about that," said Jo. "I make sure he goes home right after work and gets a good night's sleep." She gave Mother a reassuring look and pat on the hand, while throwing me a wink on the side. That seemed to satisfy both of them. They stayed for a couple of days but did not come in the Bowery again. I had dinner with them one night at their motel, and Daddy told me about the good summer they had had packing peaches. I felt guilty not having been there, and yet I knew I wouldn't have been able to get along with Dick, and anyway, he was the son that Daddy really needed at that time.

There was another aspect of this that didn't hit me until later. I wonder if it ever occurred to my parents that the boy-man on stage at The Bowery was just a younger version of what they were. Daddy's jokes and stories, Mother sitting down at the piano and singing while Daddy would accompany her on the banjo, both of them winging their way through the old songs while their Williamston friends would sing along with them in our living room and laugh and clap their hands. Playing at The Bowery, I was merely singing a different chorus of the same song they had been singing for years, but in my own key and rhythm, rather than theirs. It is a gift, of course—the ability to do this—but I would not come to understand this until much later in my life. When you're nineteen, life is a blast, a gas, a ball, and everything is *so* cool.

All too soon, Labor Day rolled around, and it was time to pull up stakes and head back to college. It was the summer of a lifetime—one I was destined to repeat again and again in a hundred different ways and towns and clubs for the next ten years, all across America. Thinking back now, if during that time, anyone had tried to engage me in a conversation about God, I would have done anything to change the subject. This is why I can understand why today's young people are so distant from anything that even remotely resembles a personal relationship with God. Today's parents agonize, weep and wail, wondering when their children will see the light. The thing is: you cannot receive God until you ask for Him, for He does not force Himself upon you.

Moreover, it is in the very act of this asking that the seeds of redemption sprout, take root and grow. But for these people I speak of—the lost ones—God is the last thing they want to think about. Worse yet, the temptations today are far greater than they were then. Beer and/or Jack Daniels was my limit, but booze wasn't really where it was at for me. I was high on some hundred and twenty proof stuff called life in the raw. I could never get enough of it, and I knew that I could not nor *would* not ever go back to Williamston. My boyhood was at an end. Hungers and appetites had been awakened in me that would drive me for years to come. Dominate me. Finally—all but destroy me.

But at the time, who cared?

•

CHAPTER
7

Ten years blew by in a storm of self.

The hurricane season of my soul.

I caused my family headaches, heartaches, pains in the neck and elsewhere. I enlisted in the army and loved the physical challenge and adventure, but found out I didn't take regimentation too well and got out with an Honorable Discharge. (I think we were both glad to get rid of each other.) Understand now: I wasn't the black sheep of the Levin family—maybe something closer to polka dot pink or fire engine red, which incidentally, was the color of the big Harley that I jumped on after graduating college and rode all the way across America. I worked as a "roughneck" in the big oil strike in west Texas, was a short order cook, did this, tried that, then back to graduate school in a serious way, earning my master's at the University of Iowa. Afterwards, I decided to give show business a serious shot, auditioned for Allied Artists and was "signed as a property." I bought some first class duds to wear, and entered into a whole new adventure.

Toby Gunn, my agent, booked me in piano bars up and down the coast, first in bust-out joints, working in tank towns like Owensboro, Kentucky, that were slightly improved versions of The Bowery, but as the owners would sing my praises to Toby, he would keep moving me up the ladder, working posh little clubs and sassy watering holes for the smart set. They called it "playing the circuit." Fort Walton Beach, Daytona, Atlanta, New Orleans, Cincinnati, Houston—everywhere and anywhere. I worked a duo in a club in Atlanta with a guy named Dave Madden, and we became good friends. (Dave got booked into The Little Club in Beverly Hills, was seen by a talent scout and

43

wound up on *Laugh In*—the guy with the glass of milk always tossing confetti, and later, played Reuben in *The Partridge Family*.

Wherever I was, after the gig, I would grab my trumpet, seek out some after-hours joint, walk in, introduce myself to the bartender ("Hey, I'm Ronnie, you know—working the single at The Lemon Tree Lounge") then jump up on the bar, shuck my shirt and start playing the blues. I would knock back shots of 100 proof Smirnoff burning it up like a jet does fuel; the customers would keep sending me drinks, and after about two choruses of "The Saints Go Marching In," I'd switch to after-burners and blast through the sound barrier. Then just as the sky turned pink, I'd go on automatic pilot, somehow manage to find my motel room and trundle off to bed, sometimes with a lady friend, sometimes not. Who knew? Who cared? The next thing I'd remember would be somebody pounding on the door, saying, "maid service," and I'd holler out, "Just leave the towels and come back later." So it went day after day, traveling farther and farther into the wilderness of self.

There are all kinds of drugs in this world. I never took any of those that came in vials or rocks or syringes. I got high on excitement and was addicted to any new adventure I could find. I even wound up in Havana the night Castro invaded the city with his army of *Fidelistas*, and I was one of the last gringos to leave before he shut it down. What I was doing there is nobody's business but mine and the Lord's. All you need to know is that it wasn't illegal or immoral, but that's another story for another time. Wherever and whenever I could find a new adventure, I'd go for it. The riskier, the better.

Finally, when I had burned out on all those smoky bars and the rest of that dark world that comes alive after the sun goes down, I'd drop out of time, rent some cottage on a wintry beach, or down in the back country of Mexico, forget all about night clubs and hole up with books and my typewriter: pondering, searching for answers that never came. I believed in the existence of a divine being, but more as the creator of nature, and that was it. There was no knowledge of a *living* God. No relationship.

44

No dialogue. I didn't know there was a Holy Spirit that could breathe the warm breath of life into my soul. That wonderful Hebrew word: *ruach!*

God was a nice abstract. A pleasant concept. Beyond that—zip.

In the summer, I would work with my father and Dick at Valley View Farms, at Campobello, SC, where by now we had our own peach trees growing, though they were still too young to bear fruit. Daddy and I would call on growers all over the county to buy their peaches, and in the process, he and I began to form a real relationship for the first time in our lives. I'd tramp over those red clay hills and gradually learned to estimate exactly what an orchard would yield. Then I'd come back to where daddy and the farmer were sitting on the front porch sipping fresh lemonade or iced tea. I'd slip daddy a little note with the numbers on it, he'd glance at it, then start bargaining with the grower. Dick made the packing house run like a Swiss watch, and it all worked. Daddy created a brand called "Drippin' Honey" which was distinctive because in the top of every basket of peaches was a little jar of honey. The brand became famous—in its way as well known in the peach industry as indeed Chiquita was to bananas or Sunkist to lemons. "Honey's" always brought more than the competing brands did, and though I didn't realize it then, Meyer Levin was a marketeer before anybody knew what the word meant.

Finally, in the fall of 1963, while living in a tobacco barn out in the country from Chapel Hill, I met a lovely young woman who was in school at Duke, and on July 4th of the next year, we were married. Through a chance encounter with the Dean of Spartanburg Junior College (now Spartanburg Methodist) I was offered a teaching job starting in the fall. Not long after I came on board, I met and became friends with Jim Hunter, a young teacher and chaplain, and we hit it off from the very first moment we met. I was the first and only Jew ever to teach there, but if it made any difference to my students, they gave no notice of this, though the administration was a somewhat different story. (You'll have to ask Jim about that.) Though the year was challenging and

45

demanding—even draining at times—teaching those bright-eyed, eager kids was far more fulfilling than playing for drunks in smoke-filled lounges.

At three in the morning on March 23, 1965, after a nip and tuck race with time and a breech birth going wrong, Sally gave birth to our wonderful daughter, Gretchen. We will always be grateful to the surgeon who pulled a miraculous save at the last minute. He told me later that ten minutes more, and Gretchen would have been lost to us forever.

Sally, Gretchen and I would go to dances that I booked around the area, while our little two-month-old girl lay there in a picnic hamper beside the piano, her eyes fixed on Daddy standing up there with his trumpet doing "the Saints." Then summer came, and I was up north promoting our brand in the wholesale produce markets with a slide show, brochures—the whole nine yards. Starting at midnight in New York, I'd go to Philadelphia, Boston and sometimes even Cleveland. This kind of marketing had never been done before, and it helped drive up the demand for Drippin' Honey peaches, and made our brand a specialty, not a commodity, and that meant top dollar from the major chain buyers.

Later that same summer, a seemingly random incident occurred in the life of my father that still today is making itself felt, some thirty years later. It was August, the packing season was over, and Daddy had come back from a trip up to the northern markets. We were having breakfast, and he was telling me about an interesting man he just happened to sit next to on the flight back to Spartanburg from New York. His name was Gene Stone—to be precise, Eugene E. Stone III.

Daddy told me that Gene was founder and owner of a mammoth apparel plant in Greenville that made children's wear and other lines as well. He and Gene had hit it off together during the flight, Daddy telling him all about the farm, and for that reason, my father wanted me to drive to Greenville and bring Gene a gift box of fancy peaches. I had no desire to meet this man, but Daddy persisted, saying I would really like him.

He took note of my reluctance and said, "Well, if you don't

46

want to go, I'll just have to do it myself, and I don't have the time." That always worked with me, and he knew it. Accordingly, I picked out a special basket and drove the thirty miles to Greenville to deliver the fruit, grumbling all the way.

Gene Stone was a living legend in the apparel industry, as I was to discover. He and his charming wife, Linky, along with the help of a handful of loyal, hardworking young women, had started the business just as the depression got under way. The fact that he managed not only to survive but succeed was a tribute to his energy and zeal as well to Linky's being there as his strong right arm, plus the loyalty of those who worked with him all those years. Eventually, I was to learn that he not only knew his stuff in what was a tough, dog-eat-dog business, he also had enough charm to fill the Braves stadium, powered as he was by a mega charge of voltage and enthusiasm. Gene showed me around the complex, and I got to say hello to his son, Jack, though we barely had time to exchange greetings before his father whisked me off to complete the tour. He told me to thank my father for the peaches and said that my dad really impressed him.

"Your father told me on the plane how you've been promoting your peaches up north, and I was impressed. I could use a man with your talents around here."

"Well, why don't you give me a job then?" It came out of me before I knew I had even said it.

He adopted that stern visage that I would come to recognize as his trademark when he became serious with someone, and the sparkle in his eyes turned into a steely glint that wouldn't let you go.

"Now, Ron, you already *have* a job. You stay with your father because he needs you there at the farm."

At that moment, little did I know that just six months later on a cold and grey January afternoon, Dick was to call from Chapel Hill and say just two words that would pierce my heart like an icicle.

"Daddy's dead."

An aneurysm had struck without warning. In those days, regrettably, diagnosis for this kind of thing was not what it is today.

47

After that, it was never the same. I realized that Valley View Farms and Drippin' Honey peaches had always been Daddy's dream, not mine. We managed to bring in the crop that summer, and then when the last peach had been picked and packed, financing for the next year's crop was out of the question. We owed the minority stockholders too much money—one of the great dangers of starting a business undercapitalized—and we knew we would have to turn it over to them.

One morning, as I sat out in the orchard in the Bronco, Gene Stone's words were echoing in my ear: *I could really use a good man like you.*

I sped over to Spartanburg and fired off a two-hundred word telegram to him. (I still have it, almost thirty years later.) Apparently it worked because it was barely two hours later that he called me, and I will never forget what he said: "Ron Levin, you rascal, you. How much did it cost you to send that thing— it's over two hundred words! Boy, you just won't do." He broke into laughter. Then he said, "Come on over. I want you to meet some of our people."

The next morning I was grilled by a half-dozen of his management team, and they said they'd think about it. I called both my brothers and told them about the offer, and my eldest brother, Bob, said three things:

First, he won't hire you because they never hired a Jew before (though they *did* have Jewish salesmen on the road). Two, he won't pay you what you're asking him, because you're not worth it. You know nothing about the business; and three, if you *do* get hired, you won't last a month. Based upon what Bob knew about me, he had every right to say that.

Gene hired me. And he paid me what I asked for.

Sally and I moved our mobile home to Greenville, setting it up in Berea, a blue collar area north of town. The year that followed was one of listening and learning, and in the process, I was able to make some genuine contributions to the company as well as forming a strong, sure friendship with Jack. Sally and I started attending Friday night services at the reform temple. She had become disenchanted with Catholicism long before having

48

met me and had converted to Judaism before our marriage. But for me, worship was no different than what I remembered from years earlier. I read the words, listened to the Rabbi, but no light came on. No fire was kindled. I would try with all my heart and mind to get into it. I would sit there, trying to feel the presence of God beside me, close to me. I wanted to *know* Him. I wanted to feel joy, to be excited about God, but instead, I would leave the temple feeling guilty. I thought that God wasn't letting me come to Him because I was doing something wrong. Something bad. Maybe my past life was catching up with me. All those years in show business, the booze, the women, the whatever—and now I was having to pay the price. Did He want me to atone for that?

If so—how? I didn't have a clue.

The one thing I *did* know after a while was that I wanted to be out on my own. Stone had been wonderful to me, but it was time to move on. I had looked at the level of work being done by the few ad agencies in Greenville and knew I could do better, just as Meyer Levin had once known he could grow and pack better peaches than the people who had been doing it for a generation or more. I shared my thoughts and feelings with Gene and Jack, and though they wanted me to stay, they saw how determined I was, wished me well, and I was out the door.

Sally took a job in a department store selling shoes for seventy-five cents an hour. I hung out my shingle, found a printer named Ravenel Scott who printed my business cards, and bingo, I was in business, calling myself Ronnell, Inc. I had an eight by ten office on Wade Hampton underneath a dentist named Dr. Butcher. I leased a typewriter, had a phone installed, and my total monthly overhead was thirty-four dollars. Cracking that nut would be a piece of cake. The tougher challenge would be to crack the Greenville market wide open.

Right from day one, I developed a very simple tactic. I would walk into someone's office, bring cookies for the secretary, ask to see the president, telling her I had something very important to tell him and no one else. She'd get me in, and I'd stand there before his desk and say: "Mr. Kendrick, my name is Ron Levin, and you don't know me, but I've got the best marketing ideas in

Greenville. Give me ten minutes to prove it, and if you don't like what you hear, throw me out!"

It worked.

Within days, I was shooting about 90% from the line, and Ronnell was off and running.

Flat out!

8

one became Group 4

Ronnell joined forces with an art studio after a year, and after landing a couple of prestigious, high visibility clients and creating attention-getting, award-winning campaigns for them, we had both Carolina's buzzing with excitement and took off, blazing a trail in the marketplace like a comet.

Additionally, we changed our name to Group Four and before long began being recognized nationally for our brand of creative excellence, including a handful of prestigious ANDY's from the Advertising Club of New York, something no small southern advertising agency had ever done before. All this was possible because high energy, keen-minded, gifted people came to us eager to sign on for the trip, and my role was one of pathfinder: the guy who would go after the business, bring it on home, then supply the creative impetus. A hybrid of Luke Skywalker and Johnny Appleseed out there in the hustings. Here's where all the lessons from Meyer Levin came into play, and did I ever need them. The agency excited me enormously, and tragically, apart from spending time with Gretchen, there was nothing else in my life. I worked, slept, ate and dreamed Group Four. I would target a client I wanted us to have, go after them and would not let up until they were "in the house." Imagine a Russian-Jewish bulldog with the personality of a standard poodle, and you get the idea.

Jerry Della Femina, one of the legendary greats in the business, once made the memorable remark that "Advertising is the most fun you can have and still keep your clothes on." Was he ever right. It is the most seductive, indeed, addictive business I know. Worse yet, it can possess you like nothing else you've ever known, which explains why ad people have a high level of divorce. Many drink too much, also, though nowadays, it's drugs as well. But against the panoply of all this high drama and adventure, the free wheeling creative highs and all nighters before presentations, the indescribable, cork-popping thrill of coming back with the account in your pocket—beyond all of this, there is a painful side to it that most people in the industry won't talk about, but I will.

The sad fact is that other professionals perceive advertising people as nothing more than glorified, creative versions of business prostitutes. I once had an overstuffed banker tell me he wanted an ad done his way, and I told him he was wrong and explained why, but it didn't matter. He just laughed and said, "You ad guys are all whores—you'll do anything for money." I wouldn't and didn't. I subsequently resigned the account, and that was my reputation in the business. I was hard-headed enough not to allow clients to dictate to us, nor would I allow them to treat our people badly and deny them the respect they deserved. Some clients couldn't deal with this; others could, and grew to respect us.

More importantly, in all my years in the business, I do not believe I met more than a half-dozen people who even mentioned God, let alone wanted to talk about Him in any serious way. Oh, they might have gone to church or synagogue, but I have long since learned that one's doing that is hardly evidence of a personal, intimate relationship with God. A passing knowledge, yes, but often, no more. But if God was out of the picture, we were definitely *in* it—full screen. We were what is known in the trade as a "hot shop," and things couldn't have been any better.

Four years passed, and then one day while driving down to Atlanta, I stopped, as I frequently did, for a sausage biscuit at a place called Katherine's Kitchen. They had been there for years, and I always wondered why they had never rolled the concept out on a grand scale. Suddenly, while driving back to Greenville, the idea hit me and I pulled off the road so I could collect the thoughts racing around in my head. I could see it all, as though I were looking at a hologram. There was a little yellow house like

Grandma used to have, with shutters, a railed porch, a picket fence, flowers, inside all the charm and warmth of what I had remembered from Williamston. We'd serve ham, steak and sausage biscuits, and the packaging and uniforms and everything would evoke strong memories in people who had grown up in the south.

I would call it . . *Miz Biskit!*

Stand by to launch! Ron L. was at it again.

Happily, my partner was as excited as I was, and others caught the fever as well. We did conceptual drawings, hired an architect, rented a piece of land, built the building, put together the menu, the packaging, an advertising campaign to launch it, found two men to run it for us, who proclaimed themselves to be operations professionals, and within three months we had our grand opening. It was an instant hit from day one. The word spread fast, and industry leaders from other fast food chains came to see the wonder on South Pleasantburg Drive and take photos and notes, as I was later to learn. Bear in mind that in 1972, not one fast food restaurant was offering breakfast biscuits. Five years later, they all were.

Regrettably, my partner and I knew as much about running a restaurant as Pinchas Zuckerman does about picking a five-string banjo. Marketing yes; operations, no. Of course, we didn't *know* that we didn't know. No matter. Miz Biskit was succeeding in spite of that. An investment group said the concept was well on its way toward becoming the hottest new idea in the industry, and it was time to put together a franchise package. After a year or so, we would go public, they said, or someone would want to buy us out. Numbers were tossed around. Big enough to make me dizzy. Meetings and presentations for investors were set up, and we were all set to rock and roll. Until one morning in early November.

I had just finished shaving when the phone rang. The manager said, "Boss, you better get down here fast. Something's happened."

Now I realize what I am about to relate to you may sound like something your four-year-old daughter comes to you and says:

53

"Mommy . . . Daddy, there's a monster in the front yard, and he won't let me get on my tricycle." Well, this wasn't a monster like that, but perhaps something worse. I'm sure a lot of people in Greenville will remember the story . . . .

At seven-thirty that morning, the driver of a Winn Dixie tractor trailer had parked his rig at the top of the hill in the median of South Pleasantburg Drive, set his brakes, and had gone into McDonald's to get a cup of coffee. While he was inside, his brakes failed, and the huge truck rolled down the hill some two hundred feet, picked up momentum, left the street and scored a direct broadside on Miz Biskit's lovely little house. The impact was so hard that it literally knocked the house off its foundations. When I arrived, I stood outside, trying to take it all in. I walked inside to discover that the truck's cab had gone right through the wall and was now poking its ugly snout into the dining room. By the grace of God (see, I know what that means now) no one was hurt, but I was devastated.

I could tell you about insurance settlements, delays, procrastinations, fear, doubt, dismay—but let's cut to the chase. By the time, far too long, that all the litigation was settled and we re-opened, something was missing. We had added chicken to boost our lunches, but I'm not talking about a product. It was like a heart transplant that won't start beating again. Everything was in place, but it wasn't working. It is a hard fact of business that the best idea in the world is worthless without proper execution. We needed someone to ramrod it who was a food operations whiz, and that was the error. We'd hired amateurs and paid the price.

The business stumbled. It faltered. It would sputter and catch and promise to take off and then stall. Investors grew cool. The franchise people pulled back. I saw my dream vanish before my very eyes, but since it was my partner's money, I had very little if any say so at that point. Gradually, a sea change came over me. I began to lose interest in all of it: the agency, Miz Biskit, and shortly thereafter, my marriage went on self-destruct.

The glory years of our early triumphs at Group Four could not sustain us. We were still generating good work, but it was just not the same. Where there had been harmony, there was friction. What had once been a team now became a fractional group bent on internal power plays. Suspicion gave way to fear, bickering gnawed at us daily, and nothing can kill a business faster. I kept bringing in clients and doing good work, but the fire had gone out, and I knew it. In a word, it was no longer fun. This once wonderful, amazing toy was broken, and worse yet, something in me was broken as well. For all my talent and savvy, I had to admit a terrible fact to myself.

I didn't know how to fix it.

I didn't even have a clue.

At this moment, there may be those of you reading this who find yourselves in a similar situation. If any of what I have told you thus far begins to ring a bell, and you are feeling anxious about yourself, your life, your business—please know this: unless you have a strong, vibrant, personal relationship with your Creator, there is *always* going to be something broken within you. You can try to sublimate it through work as I did, drown it in alcohol (and only wind up pickling your liver), hide it through drugs or promiscuous sex, buy things and more things, travel—whatever. Choose from one or all of the above or adopt any other masking device you can afford, but the end result will always be the same. The truth of what you are will ultimately make itself known to you. And at that point, unless you are prepared and willing to *accept* that truth, on your knees before God and come to Him ready, willing and eager, then it won't work. There are no shortcuts either. Anything else you might try winds up being aspirins and Band-Aids. Talent will not save you. Intelligence will not save you. Fame will not save you. Success will not save you.

Of course, I didn't know any of this yet.

The one fact I *did* know was that the very thing I had given life to had now turned on me and was about to devour me alive.

I had to get out.

55

CHAPTER

9

In September, I was invited to come down to the University of Georgia and deliver a guest lecture, and I readily accepted. The students were starved to talk to someone from the front lines where all the action was, and as a result of that, I was offered a position on the faculty. I accepted without hesitation, for I knew I was ready to leave Group Four. I also decided I would take a few graduate courses in counseling and family psychology. I returned to Greenville and told my partner I was leaving. He looked at me and said, "You mean for the weekend?" I said no.

"For good."

When I told Gretchen, she decided to move back to Charleston with her mother, thinking she would be happier there with former childhood friends than she would be with me living in an apartment in Athens, and I agreed with her. That same weekend, a crisp, clear, golden Saturday afternoon, the phone rang. It was Jack. I had not seen him in two years or more, though I had heard he had left his family's company and gone to California to attend Stanford. As is often the case with strong fathers and sons in business together, conflict can arise, and when that happens, in order to keep the family intact, the sensible and caring thing to do is for one or the other to step aside, and that's exactly what Jack did.

We talked, and I shared my plans with him and why I was leaving the business. He told me that he was head of Levi Strauss for the Western Hemisphere (excluding the U.S.) and that he wanted me in his words "to think about Levi's." He went on to say that here were all these millions of young people all over the

57

hemisphere. What was happening in their world now and what lay ahead? How did jeans in general and Levi's in particular play to this? I was to do research and present my findings in the form of a creative presentation at Caracas, Venezuela, early in January.

The challenge set me on fire, and I started to learn all I could about what was happening with young people in their values, attitudes and life-styles as a function of what they wore. What could be done to lend strong impetus to Levi's in their opening new markets in South America; what strategies and tactics might prove helpful. I presented my findings to the group two months later, and as a result of the fee I earned for this, I was able to get through the spring semester at the university.

With the advent of summer, I wound up in San Francisco with Levi's as an in-house marketing honcho. LS&C, as they are known in the trade, had brought in a man to head up the International Division—a man whose leadership style was rather heavy-handed—at times, dictatorial, something that did not sit well with Jack or any of his team. The result is that in January of 1976, Jack accepted a position as president of a well-known sportswear firm in the L.A. area called Hang Ten that had been having some problems. And that was how I came to move to the Los Angeles area, specifically La Verne, one of a cluster of communities some thirty miles east of L.A. which included Claremont and Ontario, the latter being the headquarters of Hang Ten.

Gretchen flew out to visit with me during Christmas vacation, and we had a grand time together. She was almost twelve, and we did Disney Land up right, treasuring every moment of our time together. As New Year's approached, I hated to see her go, but I had the feeling that one day we would be together permanently: father and daughter.

The year at Hang Ten was one of enormous activity and positive accomplishment. The company had been in desperate need of leadership, and self-confidence, and Jack was able to re-kindle these fires within the people and lend impetus to the operation. Sales and profits rose dramatically, even with a major manufacturing plant burning down, and we both felt good about

58

what we were doing. That summer, Gretchen came to stay with me for a time, and as always, we cherished every moment we were together. The times, they were golden.

Now while this was happening, the born-again Christian movement was really taking off, but of course, everyone knew that Californians were nuts to start with, so this was to be expected. Face it: that's the place that saw the birth of the country's first drive-in church in Garden Grove, started by an unknown yet innovative preacher by the name of Robert Schuller, who was said by rival pastors to be so far out over the edge, he was halfway to China. Of course, since time began, people have always been saying that about those who come along with a new idea, whether it concerns God, gravity, or that box in the corner of the family room that shows pictures. Case in point: in 1925, a man walked into the offices of the *London Daily Express* and asked if he could show his invention to the editor. Upon hearing the man was downstairs, the editor called security and said: "For God's sake, go down to reception and get rid of a lunatic who just came in. He says he's got a machine for seeing pictures by wireless. Watch him—he may have a knife and be dangerous."

The man was John Baird, the inventor of television!

I began to come into contact with a few people who were authentic in their born-again lives and quite open about it. One of these was a young woman named Gail Ressel. She wasn't syrupy or gushy in the manner of a Tammy Faye, nor did she force her faith upon you. It was simply there, as a vital and natural part of her everyday life and made itself evident in the way she interacted with those around her. Throughout that fall, we would have occasional conversations about it, but as a Jew, any discussion about Jesus made me very nervous, if not downright hostile. As I would explain to Gail, Jesus had been the reason I kept getting beat up as a kid, and I wanted nothing to do with Him. She would nod and smile, then drop it. But in several days or a week, she would pick up the conversation where we left off. I really didn't mind since she was a good friend. Besides, I wasn't taking any of this seriously. To me, everything about the Christian myth was just that—an entertaining myth, and nothing more.

59

The end of the year rolled around, and Jack told me it was clear to him that because of the growing pressures and changes in the marketplace it was essential he return to the family business and lend a hand if they were to remain competitive. Gene had flown out to L.A., they had talked, and the upshot of all this was that Jack would leave Hang Ten and rejoin Stone Manufacturing. It's just as well, for we were both becoming increasingly aware that the management style at Richton, our corporate parent, had begun to show disturbing similarities to what we had seen becoming intrenched in the international division at Levi. By contrast, Jack's leadership style has always been to teach, train, support, then empower others to execute the plan. At the same time a leader has a firm hand on the throttle, the other hand must always be on the pulse of his people to make sure they remain in sync with each other and their goals.

Shortly after New Year's, Jack left Hang Ten, and I did likewise, though deciding to stay right where I was and open up—well, what else? A marketing firm. An ad agency. It's what I knew best, and though I was in the most competitive marketplace in America, it was the only real option I had at the time. I chose the name, The Bottom Line, and to my surprise and delight, the name had not yet been registered in California. I sublet a small office in a metal building located in an industrial office park in San Dimas, a scant ten minutes from the apartment. My office was about the size of a good walk-in closet but that's all I needed. The rest of the space was leased by a direct mail company headed by a genial, easy-going man named Shorty Feldbush who was 6'6", which explains how he got his nickname. He gave me a few small projects that kept me in groceries, but there wasn't really much happening. Then a man heard about me and commissioned me to write one of those long full-page advertisements that you used to see years ago in newspapers along the lines of "How I Became a Millionaire Without Investing Any of My Money." I checked the guy out, and he was legitimate in his claims, so I wrote the ad, and it ran and made him even more money than he already had, but it didn't do much for me. The result was that he wanted to hire me to work for him full time and do a whole series

60

of these, but I wanted to remain independent, for after my experiences at Levi and Hang Ten, I knew that I just wasn't cut out to work for anyone else.

After a month or so, the last salary check from Hang Ten was about gone, and my business was limping along with a few small things to do of no consequence. I was barely earning enough to pay my bills and send money back east every month for Gretchen. I began to grow more and more pessimistic about my little agency, and one day while glancing through a newspaper, I noticed an ad: *Pizza Parlor for sale in good, growing area. Profitable business. Easy to learn. We will teach you.* Just as with Miz Biskit, something hit me, and I said to myself, I have to check this out. I drove down to the location and after spending the better part of an afternoon and evening there, decided I would buy The Pizza Parlor though of course, I had no money whatsoever. The price was $7,500. No real estate included: just the business and equipment.

I worked around the clock to develop a marketing plan that I could present to the bank, showing how I intended to grow the business, offer new items, cater to office and professional people for lunch and attract families in the evening by playing piano, putting in game machines in a room and so on. When it was finished, I went to the local office of the Bank of America and presented it to the manager. I had diagrams, traffic counts, a competitive analysis of other restaurants and so forth. Finally, I had a simple daily journal from the owners on which they appeared to have kept a careful record of their receipts and expenses.

The manager heard me out very patiently, and finally I got to the page that showed how much money I needed. Seven thousand five hundred dollars for the owners and $2,500 for operating capital to get me started. I finished, clasped my hands in my lap and sat back fully confident of his answer.

"Mr. Levin," he said, "First of all, let me compliment you on such an outstanding presentation." I started to feel better already.

"You certainly went to a lot of trouble to put all this together. Very professional—it's clear you've had some experience in things of this sort. However, let me suggest you look at it from our standpoint. You have no experience, no collateral, no money of your own, no income, no property that you own, no net worth. In light of all that, do you really expect this bank to loan you ten thousand dollars to buy a pizza parlor in Chino?"

I met his glance head on. "Of course."

"Well," he said. "I have to admire your determination and your enthusiasm, but I also have to turn you down. Please understand, it's nothing personal, and I would be less than honest if I didn't tell you that my guess is, other banks will give you the same response. I'm sorry."

He indicated with a wave of his hand that our little chat was over, and I gathered together my presentation and headed for the door. Once outside, I took a deep breath of air and found myself more determined than ever that somehow, I would get the money.

I went back to the office and in desperation called Gail to see if she had any ideas of her own. She said she did and she would meet me after work, and we would talk about it. That lifted my spirits slightly, but I sat in the office going over and over the numbers and wondering if it would be worthwhile to talk to another bank, then finally decided against it. Shorty came in and said he needed me to write a letter for a direct mail campaign for a woman selling knitting yarns out of her home. Me? Ron L. the Great. The man who had created award-winning ads that ran in *The Wall Street Journal* and *Time* and *Fortune* and everywhere else. I swallowed my pride and said sure, I'd do it for him. He was a nice guy and was only trying to help me. Besides that, I needed the money.

Suddenly, Jack's face swam into view. Of course. I'd call him and ask for his help. I punched the number and after waiting a minute or so, outlined the plan to him, then waited for his answer, which was not long in coming. *Jack*

"No! Absolutely not. I will not loan you any money to buy a pizza parlor. Stay and grow your business. It's what you do best." He said he had to take another call, and I hung up. His answer just raised the ante. "Okay," I thought to myself. "I'll

62

show Jack and the Bank of America and whoever else didn't believe in me."

At five-thirty, I left and went back to the apartment to meet Gail. It was late afternoon and we sat on a green, wooden bench, the waning sun still warm on our faces and the wind picking up that wonderful perfume from the abandoned orange grove that lay behind the apartments.

"Okay," she said, her eyes dancing. "Now tell me all about this restaurant you want to buy." I did, and when I finished, she said, "And how much do you need?"

"Ten thousand dollars."

She laughed. "Is that all?"

I didn't get it. "Do you have an angel waiting in the wings?" I used the term as it's used in show business: someone who comes in as the principal backer of a film or project to bail out someone in need.

"I have someone even better."

I could hardly wait. "Gail," I said, "don't keep me in suspense. Is it someone you know? Someone willing to help me?"

She nodded, her face a wreath of smiles.

"Someone with money?"

"Well, not exactly," she said, "but then again, maybe yes."

"Who, Gail, who? Tell me." I grabbed her hands. She looked at me and smiled the way children smile at you when they're about to whisper a secret in your ear. "Oh, you dummy," she said.

"It's God. God is going to help you, Ron!"

10

I was so put out with Gail that if she hadn't been such a good friend, I would have walked away and left her sitting on the bench.

"God," I said, raising my eyebrows and nodding benignly as you would to a drunk or someone senile.

"Yes," she said. "God. And tonight, you're going to pray and ask God for help."

I sat there and looked at her for what seemed like an eternity, trying to find something—anything—in her face to indicate this was some kind of joke. Surely, this was her way of helping me to lighten up. But her eyes remained fixed on mine, her lips pursed in that way that said, I mean business.

"Gail, look, I know you're trying to be helpful and all that, but I don't need to be converted or born again or whatever. I just need ten thousand dollars. Real money. Okay?"

She wore a hurt expression on her face. "Ron, let me ask you something. Are we friends?"

"Sure."

"Good friends, right?"

"Yes, very good friends. Gail, you know that."

"Okay. Now would I do anything to hurt you?"

"No."

"So do me one favor. Don't fight me on this. You've tried the bank, and like you said, the others won't be much different, and Jack won't loan you the money, so now all you have is God, and I want you to pray to Him tonight and ask Him for help."

"You mean ask Him for ten thousand dollars."

"Not necessarily. Maybe God doesn't *want* you to have that

pizza parlor. Did you ever consider that?"

"Oh, so now you're against me."

"Oh, Ron, nobody is against you. I'm just saying that you should ask God for a sign, that's all. To give you direction."

I sat there in stony silence, chewing on my upper lip.

"Ron, when is the last time you prayed. Like, really prayed?"

"I ... don't know. It's been so long ago I can't remember."

"Well, Mister Wonderful Super Genius, would it absolutely kill you to talk to God tonight and ask for His direction? I mean— is it that painful for you?" Her eyes narrowed, and she took hold of my wrists. "Is it, huh?"

"No, no. It's not painful ... it's just. ..."

"You don't believe, do you?" Her voice dropped to a whisper.

"No, I don't ... or ... Gail, I'm not sure. I don't know if I believe or not. Right now, I'm not sure of anything anymore."

"Okay, that's a good starting place. Tonight, when everything is quiet and settled down, I want you to talk to God as though it's the first time you've ever met Him, and I want you to tell Him everything that's on your mind ... what you need, what you intend to do, then ask Him for His help. To give you a signal. Okay?"

I thought she was not only naive, but a little nuts in the bargain, but she was my friend, so I agreed.

"You promise you'll pray?" she said.

"I promise."

"Okay." We stood up, she gave me a big hug and walked toward her car. I went upstairs and kept saying to myself, I need ten thousand dollars. I *have* to have ten thousand dollars.

Later that night, I took a shower, got into my pajamas and sat down on the floor, leaning against the side of the bed. I kept thinking about what Gail had said, and without realizing it, I began talking and before I knew it, I was pouring out the story of my whole life to someone, I didn't know who, but I was calling Him God. I remember saying that after all I had accomplished, I felt like a failure. There was so much wrong with the way things were. I wanted and needed Gretchen to come live with me—we

66

needed each other. After talking for a long while, I found myself weeping hysterically. Then, the last thing I remember saying was, "Lord, tell me what to do . . . show me." Then I went to bed.

I remember the dream: I saw myself as a tiny baby sitting on someone's lap with another infant sitting next to me. I awoke in the morning and felt strangely refreshed, my mind very clear, but within a few minutes, I began ruminating over the events of the previous evening, starting with my conversation with Gail and winding up with my talk with God—or praying, or whatever she wanted to call it.

This was so crazy, and the more I thought about, the sillier I felt. No. *Stupid* is how I felt. To think I could have been conned into something so ridiculous. I needed ten thousand dollars. Period. And poor Gail, she meant well, but these Christians just didn't understand how the real world worked. They really *were* Jesus freaks, just like people called them. I felt embarrassed for having put any stock in her. I showered, dressed and went into the office and had no sooner sat down behind my desk than the door opened and a man walked in.

Tall, thin, glasses, balding, somewhat stooped. Late fifties or so. I barely knew him other than his name: Al Batchelor. A retired post office clerk. He looked at me and said, "Hi, Ron. I hear you need money to buy a restaurant."

"How did you know that?"

"I don't really remember. But that's not really important right now. Exactly how much money do you need?"

I looked at him and hoped he would just go away and leave me alone. I wasn't in the mood for small talk with a man who had sorted mail and sold stamps for thirty years. I decided the best way to get rid of him was to humor him.

"Well, Al, not that much, really, just ten thousand dollars." I sat there looking at him waiting for him to leave. I was relieved when he said, "Would you excuse me for a moment?" and left the room. I stood up and starting pacing my little cell, when the door opened again, and there he stood. He walked over and handed me something without saying a word. I looked at him, looked at what he had put in my hand, read the figures, then sat down.

67

It was a personal check. Payable to Ron Levin.

For ten thousand dollars!

I remember my eyes tracing the numbers very slowly, one at a time.

"Al," I said. "I—" My mouth wouldn't work. "I can't take this. I mean, you don't even know me. I could leave town with this, go to Oregon—anywhere."

"You could . . . but you won't."

"Well, don't you need a note?"

"Well, I suppose so . . . yes." Of course, we both knew that a personal note unsecured by collateral was all but worthless, and I reminded him of that.

"Al, I don't really understand this. You're sure you want to loan me this money?"

"I'm sure."

"But why?" Always the rationalist in a world of cause and effect.

He just shrugged, then said something I thought was very funny. "Why not!"

I had learned in life when it was time to shut up and take the money. I extended my hand and we shook. "Al . . . thanks. I'll . . . well, I'll be sure to let you know how things are going."

"I'd like that," he said. "Ron, I know you'll do okay."

I dashed over to Wells Fargo bank and opened escrow. Then called Gail and told her the good news.

"See," she said, breaking into a giggle. "Oh, Ron, what did I tell you?" I had to suppress a chuckle over the phone because in light of what had happened, now she'd never stop pestering me to go to church, keep on praying, all that stuff. But who had time for any of that now? I had to get ready to take over a restaurant, and time was at a premium. There were certificates to be signed, permits to be applied for, city, county, state, background checks for the beer and wine license—the list was endless. Most important of all, I had to learn the pizza business, so I started going over to the restaurant at lunchtime and at night, and bit by bit learned the entire process.

The owner's name—we will call him "Sal"—and his son

"Tony"—had a very simple bookkeeping system for the handling of cash, which accounted for nearly all their sales. The money simply went into an ancient register that looked as though it had once belonged to James Cash Penney himself. At the end of the night, they counted it up, each took what he needed, and the rest Sal took home with him. I could never really get a handle on how much they took in, because they would swap money back and forth during the night, from cash drawer to pocket, making change for larger bills, and naturally, there was no register tape. Finally, I started counting every sale they made, and bit by bit, I discovered the discrepancy between what they said they were doing and their actual sales—about thirty percent. What they took in was enough for them, but only because they had no debt service: no note payments, rent, wages, nothing except food, supplies and utilities.

This discovery disheartened me, but my hole card was that Sal had verbally agreed to give me an option on purchasing the real estate as well, which in that growing area might be worth something someday. He said we'd take care of this when we closed escrow. The remaining two weeks flew by, and I found myself there Thursday night before the closing which was set for nine the next morning.

"Hey, Sal," I said. "Don't forget about our agreement—you know, the option to purchase the real estate."

He glowered at me. "No, no, no! I talked it over with my wife, and she don't want me to do that." He resumed rolling out the dough for a order.

"Listen, Sal, you gave me your word."

"So okay, I gave you my word. We talked, sure. Then my wife and I talked, and I changed my mind. A man has a right to change his mind, don't he? Besides, this is my property, and I can do what I want with it. You just be there in the morning at nine o'clock, and once it's yours, then *you* can worry about all this."

I went back to the apartment and went through the numbers again. There was no way it would work, and a hollow feeling settled into my stomach. I had to pay back Al on some kind of regular basis, and then there was rent, Gretchen, my car, insurance, this and that. The more I thought about it, the worse I felt. I decided to call Gail, but her line was busy, and after a few tries I got through and told her what was going on.

"Well, dear, blessed Ron, what did you do last time?"

I drew a blank. "What do you mean *last time*?"

"You know, the first time all this started. And what happened later with Al. Remember?"

"Oh, uh . . . I prayed."

"Well?"

I was silent.

"Ron, are you telling me you haven't been praying since then?" There was no anger in her voice, just disappointment.

"No."

"Not one prayer."

"Nothing."

pray

I heard her give a deep sigh. Her silence was a command.

I flushed and felt ashamed. "Okay, I know what to do." I stammered an apology into the phone, thanked her and hung up.

That night, I prayed as before. I admitted to God that I had made another mistake, thinking that I was doing the right thing, and maybe Jack had been right, but my pride had gotten in the way, and I talked about some other things that I couldn't admit to anyone, and I wound up by asking God to give me a signal. Tell me what to do. Then I fell asleep. The next morning just before seven, the phone rang.

"Ronnie, this is Sal, okay? Say, listen. I had a long talk with my wife last night, and she don't feel too good about selling you the business. Now I could hold you to the contract and take the money, but ahh, I don't know. Tony and I been thinking, and we think maybe it's worth a little more than what we're asking. You know, we don't want to sell too cheap. What I'm saying is, unless you want to fight me on this, if you meet me at the bank at nine o'clock, I'll give you your money back."

I put the phone back on the receiver and sat on the edge of the bed staring out the window. I don't know how much time passed, but suddenly I realized I had only a few minutes to shower, dress, slug down some juice and get to the bank. Once at Wells Fargo,

70

the escrow officer executed the papers while Sal sat there smoking his usual cigarette. We both signed, got up, shook hands, she put the check in my hands, and he went out the door, and just like that, it was over. I took a deep breath and let it out slowly.

Mrs. Clifton asked me if I wanted a cup of coffee, I said yes, and she asked a secretary to bring two cups. She said I looked hungry. I said I was, and she said, "We have oatmeal raisin cookies today that a customer brought in. I'll have my secretary get you some." I sat there sipping my coffee and when the cookies came, began wolfing them down, then filling Mrs. Clifton in on what had transpired. When I finished eating, I thanked her and stood up, preparing to leave.

She said, "Well, Mr. Levin, I'm sorry things didn't work out just the way you planned, but perhaps—"

A man who had been standing close by broke into our conversation.

"Excuse me, but by any chance, are you Ron Levin?"

"Yes."

Mrs. Clifton said, "Oh, Mr. Levin, this is Frank Adamson, with the county health department. We see each other a lot."

"Hey, yeah. But listen, you're the one buying The Pizza Parlor, right?"

"Well, I was." I told him the gist of what had happened.

He looked at me for a moment. "Listen, Mr. Levin, you don't know how lucky you are."

I asked him what he meant.

"Well, see, I'm head of restaurant inspections for the county, and that place has five major violations against it. We're just about to serve Mr. Salvatore with an order to put in all new bathrooms, commercial dishwasher and air conditioning, too. You wouldn't believe what we found: dead birds and rats up in the air conditioning unit on the roof; the plumbing in the floor under the toilets has to be all dug up and replaced, new lavatories, you know, the whole nine yards. I had my man come out and do a workup on everything, and he figured maybe twenty-seven, twenty-eight thousand dollars for the job."

71

I took a deep breath. "And what if Sal doesn't do this?"

"Well, he's gotta show intent to do it within the next month or so—you know, signed bids and all that, and then we'll let him keep his license."

"But what if he doesn't?"

"I'll shut him down."

"What if I had bought it, instead?"

"I would have shut you down, too. No hard feelings, but the law is very clear, and this county is hard on restaurants. Always has been."

I thanked him, said good-bye to Mrs. Clifton and walked out to my car. There was a bright sun shining, it was early April, and I felt a rush of relief and gratitude come over me. I leaned on the hood of my car and started saying, "Thank You, God. Thank You, Lord," over and over.

When I arrived back at the office, I had no sooner sat down than Al came in. He wanted to know how it went, and I told him the whole story and held out the check. "Here, I guess you want this back."

He hesitated a moment, looking into my face. "No," he said. "You keep it. You may need it for what's ahead."

"Al, believe me, there is nothing ahead. I have no business. No clients. Nothing."

"Ron, you don't really know that, do you?" He peered at me over his glasses.

I didn't follow him. "What do you mean? I know what I see, Al."

"Yes, I know. It's just that there are some things we're not given to know. Anyway, listen . . . you keep the check; of course, if it'll make you feel better to give it back, that's okay, too. Whatever works best for you."

He went out, and I sat there lost in thought. I started to run back over everything that had happened. If I had bought the restaurant, there would have been no way I could have gotten the money for the improvements in order to stay open, since it wasn't even my property; and no one was going to loan money to me to make improvements on a building that I didn't even own. I would have been bankrupt.

Now what? I thought. The bottom line for The Bottom Line was that I had a nothing ad agency going nowhere fast, and no prospects in sight.

"Oh, Lord," I said aloud. "What am I gonna do? I'm lost again." Then I thought about Gail and decided to call her to let her know the news. Just as I reached for the phone, it rang.

"Ron Levin," the voice said. "Man, I've been looking all over for you."

I recognized the voice at once. It belonged to Dr. Tom Brigham, founder of Beech Mountain and Sugar Mountain, two legendary ski resorts in the mountains of North Carolina. Under my direction, the creative team at Group Four had created the original advertising and marketing for both of these that had successfully positioned them in the marketplace and helped them take off. But I hadn't talked to Tom Brigham in over three years or so.

"Ron, I have some exciting news for you. Remember the stuff you helped me with at Snowshoe?" Tom was referring to a major ski resort that he founded in the mountains of West Virginia about three years ago. We had created the identity for Snowshoe along with their initial package of marketing materials that had been honored for their creative excellence.

"Well, look, this isn't going to be like the first time. I know we ran out of money, but now we have major financing with a twenty million dollar letter of credit from the Saudi's, and their name is as good as that black stuff that comes out of the ground. Anyway, we're off and running, and it's a brand-new ball game. But now here comes the good part: I want The Bottom Line to be our national marketing firm. The first year's ad budget is about $400,000."

"Ron? Ron . . . are you still there?"

I mumbled a yes and noticed my feet were dancing up and down, my knees shaking and my head dizzy.

"Okay, now listen. We're up in Vegas right now at the ski show, and Manny and I want you up here so we can get started. You come up tonight, and I'll have a room waiting for you in your

73

name—we're at the Sands. We'll have an early breakfast in the room and fill you in on everything. Gotta run, Ron babe. We're late for a meeting."

I couldn't wait to tell Gail. We met just as the sun was setting, and she hugged me for joy and said, "Ron, the Lord sent you an angel, and his name is Al. And God is using me, too. Just like he used Jack, and now Tom Brigham. Don't you see? The Lord is trying to tell you something, and He's doing this because He wants you to know His Son."

I told her I was grateful for what happened, but I really wasn't interested in getting to know Jesus. I didn't really believe all that Son of God stuff anyway, but I didn't want to hurt her feelings. I told her that with Snowshoe to work on, everything was going to be okay. And that one of these days, she and I would have a good long talk about God, but if He wanted me to know His Son, now that was a different matter, and He was going to have to wait a long time.

She said that was all right. I asked her why, and she said, "Because God has all the time in the world."

"And . . .?"

"And Ron . . . you don't."

With that, she hugged me, kissed me on the cheek and disappeared into the growing dusk. I went upstairs, threw some clothes together, jumped in the car and headed out on the San Bernadino freeway toward Vegas.

Snowshoe! Man, this was going to be fantastic. Life was great. I turned on the tape, opened the sun roof on the Rabbit and started singing at the top of my voice. Judy Collins. "Send in the Clowns."

Isn't it rich. . . .

CHAPTER
11

Business exploded.

No sooner had I gotten under way with Snowshoe than new clients started calling me. I was amazed. I wasn't doing anything different than before, and I certainly wasn't praying. The thought of God did enter my mind occasionally, but as far as I was concerned, all that would have to stay on the back burner.

Within a month, I had earned enough to make a down payment on a condominium just up the street on Foothill Boulevard. When I went back east for a working visit with Snowshoe, I made a stop at Raleigh-Durham, picked up a car and drove over to visit my mom at her apartment in Chapel Hill. Mother greeted me warmly and then said, with a strange look on her face, "Come on out in the backyard, I have a surprise for you." I had no idea what to expect, but there in the backyard on a blanket with a picnic lunch was Gretchen. Of course! It was her birthday, March 23! I had sent her a letter and a present, but knowing I was going to be here, she had gotten on a bus by herself and come up from Charleston to be with me. After some serious hugging, she told me that she was unhappy and wanted to come live with me. I assured her that I wanted us to be together as much as she did and that I would talk to her mother, and we would work it out.

After spending several days at Snowshoe, I returned to California to plunge into the work that had to be done if we were to meet our deadlines. I began conversations with Gretchen's mother, Sally, and after some conversation, she agreed that Gretchen should be with me and would come out when the school year was over.

While all this happening, another event began to unfold right next door. In the corner unit next to mine lived a young couple: early to mid-twenties, attractive, quiet, presentable, and though I saw them occasionally, our relationship was limited to nodding and exchanging pleasantries. Then, one Friday afternoon in early May, the woman, her name was Lisa, asked me a rather unusual question.

"Are you going to services tonight?"

She caught me off guard, and I had to stop and think for a moment. Surely, they weren't Jewish. Then why the question. I told her that no, I wasn't.

"Oh, then you're not a *practicing* Jew?"

"No, I'm not." I wondered where this was going.

"Well, if you're free, Jason and I would like you to have dinner with us tonight."

Living alone and with the schedule I had, I always welcomed a good, home-cooked meal, thus I readily accepted and at seven, showed up at their door. We chatted a bit before dinner was served, and I discovered that Jason was in seminary studying for the ministry. Lisa hailed from New Mexico, and she had met Jason when they were in college. A Vietnam veteran, he had come back from the war and after knocking around a bit, had decided to go to college, and that's where they met. She announced that dinner was ready, and we sat down at the table.

"We'd like you to pray with us," said Jason.

The three of us joined hands, and Jason prayed and he concluded the prayer by saying, " . . . and Lord, thank You for sending Ron to us. Amen."

I thought that was a bit odd but made no comment. The food was superb, and as we ate, Lisa told me the story of their courtship and all that happened since then. When she met Jason, they were immediately attracted to one another, but he was not a Christian. By contrast, Lisa had a strong faith, and this presented a real problem, and she told Jason she could never marry him until he accepted Christ. In response, he said that he wasn't about to do that since he didn't really believe in any of that stuff. I nodded, thinking how familiar that all sounded.

"Then it happened," she said. "Jason became ill and went

76

into the hospital for diagnostic tests. He was losing weight rapidly, and they couldn't figure out what was wrong."

"I had these sores that suddenly appeared all over my body," said Jason. "I thought it was some kind of bug, you know, a parasite that I picked up while in Nam, but they couldn't identify it."

"So he stayed in the hospital and continued to grow worse," continued Lisa. "I would come after work and spend the evening with him, sleeping in the chair by his bed, and it seemed that every morning when I awoke to check on him, he was growing more and more pale, losing more weight, and the sores were getting worse. The doctors had admitted to me they were stumped, and my frustration was compounded by the fact that I would ask Jason to accept Christ, and he would lie there in the bed, shake his head and stare out the window.

"Finally one night, I told him that I knew Christ loved him and that if he would only open his heart to Jesus, the power of the Holy Spirit would be able to enter his life. I became so emotional," said Lisa, "that I burst into tears, and we held each other's hands for a long while. Finally, he looked at me, and said, 'What do I have to do to accept Jesus?'

"I told him he had to ask Him for forgiveness and to confess his sins, and make a commitment to do whatever the Lord would ask him to do."

"I couldn't believe it was that simple," Jason said. "I had always fought it because . . . well, you know, I didn't want to feel like I owed anybody anything. I'd always been pretty much on my own because that was the only way I knew how to live."

Lisa went on: "I could see he had a high fever, and after the nurse came in to give him his last medicine for the night, I put cold compresses on his forehead and sat there with him, the two of us praying together, and that's the last thing I remember until morning came. I awoke to the sound of people talking, and when my eyes adjusted to the light, I saw several nurses and doctors clustered around the bed. They were talking in hushed tones, and since I couldn't see Jason, I sprang out of my chair, pushed through them and there was Jason lying very still with his eyes closed. My first thought was that during the night he had died. At least, I thought, he died having accepted Jesus, and now he was in heaven.

"Then I saw his eyelids move. I turned to the doctor who was his primary physician and said, "What is it, doctor? What's happening?"

"Well, I'm not sure," he said. "Look at this." He pulled back Jason's pajama top, and I could see the lesions were no longer their angry, red color but seemed to have lightened in hue plus decreased in their size. They had been the size of a quarter and now they had shrunk to about the size of a dime. "Also," said the doctor, his brow wrinkled, "his temperature is normal."

Then Jason opened his eyes and spoke. "Hi, honey. Boy, am I hungry!" He smiled at me, and I smiled back." Lisa paused and sipped at her coffee. "You tell the rest," she said, looking at her husband.

"Well, in three days I was out of there," said Jason, "and they pronounced me cured. The doctors were really puzzled and said I had gone into spontaneous remission."

Lisa laughed. "That's what they call it, when they don't have any other explanation."

Jason went on with the story. "Anyway, by then, the sores had all but completely disappeared, I started gaining weight and getting my strength back, and a week later, I was baptized and knew that I had been called to ministry. So we looked around for a seminary and decided to come out here and live while I went to school. Lisa's father is helping us."

Lisa got up and brought in a cake she had baked, and we munched away while sipping our coffee. It was then that she wanted to know about my life as a Jew: what it was like growing up, worshiping and so on. I gave her a brief sketch of my life, including some of the things I have told you thus far, while both of them listened with keen interest. She left the table and returned with a Bible. "Do you ever read this?" she asked.

I shook my head. "Not really." I thought, oh, no. Now we're going to have Sunday school.

"Ron, are you familiar with Isaiah?" she asked.

"Wasn't he a prophet?"

"Yes, but a very special kind." She and Jason exchanged smiles.

She opened the Bible, then looked back at me and said, "If you don't mind, let me just read you this one passage. I really want you to hear it."

I nodded, thinking to myself that this was the least I could do, having been invited for dinner. It wouldn't kill me.

"Therefore the Lord himself will give you a sign. Behold, the virgin shall conceive and bear a Son, and shall call his name Immanuel."

She looked up at me and smiled. "You never heard that before, did you?"

"No," I said. "This is all news to me. Now, just where is this?"

"Isaiah 7:14." I looked puzzled, and she said, "Chapter 7, verse 14. I'm sorry. It's just that Jason and I are so used to talking like that. You want to hear more?"

I nodded. She read from chapter 11 and skipped about in Isaiah, reading some other verses from chapter 53, equally astounding.

"When did Isaiah write all this?" I asked.

"About 750 B.C. or so," said Jason.

"We're talking about seven hundred and fifty years before the birth of Christ?"

"Right."

"And ... now let me get this straight. He was one of *our* guys, wasn't he?"

They both laughed at that.

"So this means. . . ." I didn't finish my sentence but sat there in silence, not knowing what else to say. Then something hit me from earlier in the evening. "Why did you say what you did during the prayer—about thanking God for sending me to you?"

They both started talking at once, then Jason let Lisa tell the story.

"Since the day we moved in here, we have been asking the Lord to send a Jew to live next door to us, so we could witness to him. And He sent you."

79

Immediately, my guard was up. There had to be a rational explanation. "But, surely there are other Jews living here in the condominiums."

They both shook their heads slowly.

"But—why it is so important that a Jew should . . . that you should witness to me?"

"Because we love the Jewish people," said Jason. "In fact, after I graduate seminary next June, Lisa and I are going to Israel to live and work on a *kibbutz* and bring the message of *Yeshua* to the Jews. That's His name in Hebrew," he added. "You see, Israel is the only hope of mankind, and it should be every Christian's duty to aid the Jews in their fight to maintain their homeland, for unless we do, there is no hope for the world."

I sat there in astonishment. Lisa got up and came back to refill our coffee cups. I looked up at her. "You're going to live on a *kibbutz*?" I couldn't factor this at all. We talked some more. I told them that Gretchen was going to come live with me. I told them a bit about my business, and then a thought occurred to me.

"Listen, since you're moving, when you sell your condominium, I'd like the chance to buy it. I could move into this one and rent out mine—Gretchen and I will need the extra bedroom when she comes to live with me."

Now these were the days of the incredible real estate boom in southern California, and people would literally camp out for three days waiting for new homes to go on sale. Jason told me they had already promised it to someone else, and he only wished they had known earlier. I told them that was okay—that two months ago I didn't even have money to put gas in my car. I just thought I'd ask, but it wasn't that important.

When I got ready to call it a night, Lisa said, "Do you have a Bible?"

I told her I didn't, and she said, "Then I want you to have this one. Please, it's important to me." I took it, thanked her and hugged them both then went next door and lay the Bible down on my bedside table. That night, I found it hard to get to sleep, so I sat up in bed, opened the book and thumbed through it until I came to the chapter she had read from. I read it over and over, then turned to the beginning of the chapter and began to read about this man called Isaiah. I read the entire book, and when I finished I lay there in bed wondering about what I had read. How could he have known all this, and if he was prophesying this to the Jews, why didn't they listen? I finally fell asleep and when I awoke the next morning, Isaiah was the last thing on my mind.

Business came first.

Hardly a month had passed when I heard a knock on my door and opened it to find Jason and Lisa there. "We just wanted to tell you," said Jason, "that our friend who was wanting to buy our unit couldn't get his financing straight, so if you want it, it's yours. We just want out of it what we have in it." I couldn't believe my ears. Gretchen was coming out soon to stay, and everything seemed to be falling into place. My business was making enough money now that I could easily come up with the down payment, and within three weeks, we had closed the deal. I moved in next door and found a tenant for my other unit that same weekend.

I could not believe my good fortune. Three months ago, it appeared that Gretchen would not be able to come live with me. I had no clients. No business. No chance. And now, my daughter was coming to live with me permanently, I owned two condominiums that were appreciating in value almost daily. Business was flourishing, so much so that I was about to move into new and larger office space and hire a full-time assistant. I wondered what I had done to deserve all this. Clearly, I hadn't been praying. I certainly hadn't accepted Christ. Therefore, it couldn't be that. Then what did it mean? Finally, I came to the conclusion that things just happened, whether you believed or prayed or not.

After all, if good things happened to one on the basis of one's belief in God and accepting Jesus, then I really didn't deserve any of this.

Right?

CHAPTER

12

Gretchen

The happiest day for me in years occurred that summer when I stood at the gate at LAX, and saw my daughter coming off the plane. We ran toward each other and after a minute of serious hugging, picked up her baggage and started for home. She was to be with me permanently now, and all the wrangling and waiting and wondering were over.

Business wise, good things continued to happen. The Bottom Line grew, and soon I was able to purchase an old house on a high traffic corner in Claremont. I renovated the house into office space, and now I owned two condominiums and an office building. Not long afterwards, the dean of the graduate school of Claremont offered me a teaching position in the School of Business. My students were in the MBA program, a keen-minded group, and teaching them proved to be a welcome respite from the rigors and pressures of the day. The faculty was top-notch; in fact, right across from my office was one of the most respected authorities in management and marketing: Peter Drucker.

As the school year began for Gretchen, it became readily apparent that the public school she was attending in La Verne left a lot to be desired. Fights were commonplace, drugs were taking hold, she felt threatened, and I knew this was no way to start off a new home and new school year for her. The only alternative, however, was a parochial school, Our Lady of the Assumption, that was in Claremont. Gretchen and I paid a visit to Sister Mary Seraphine, the director, inquired about an opening, but she was less than enthusiastic that the Father would accept Gretchen as a student. After all, she explained, "There was a waiting list of

83

students who were Catholic, and. . . ." She looked at me, her glance finishing the sentence. She understood how serious the situation was in the public schools and said she would pray for the right decision to be made. A week later, Sister Seraphine called; the answer was yes. Gretchen entered "Our Lady" and we both breathed a sigh of relief.

Gretchen had something of a rocky road at first and couldn't seem to settle down, to fit into the groove. Whatever rebelliousness I saw in her I knew had to be a residue of anger left over from all the bad experiences she had been through in which she had been largely powerless. Sister Seraphine detected the problem early on and called a meeting with me, Gretchen and her teachers. The sisters were caring yet candid: no punches pulled. Gretchen and I listened as they told her what changes she would have to make or else. After the meeting, we talked about it briefly, and she told me she had made a promise to herself that she would make it work. Whatever thought processes the meeting had generated, it apparently accomplished its desired objective, for she straightaway settled down and became a happy and productive student.

The next two years were pleasant ones for both of us. Gretchen enjoyed school, made friends, and I kept building the business and juggling that with parenting. Incidentally, one afternoon, I happened to find myself only a block or two away from the old pizza parlor that I had almost bought. I stopped in and by chance, the new owner was there. I told him who I was, and he remembered my name and confessed to me that in the first three months after buying it, he had invested just under thirty thousand dollars in improvements. He was killing himself working eighty hours a week, and at this very moment was trying to find a buyer for it—though, he added, without much luck. I walked out of there into the bright sunshine and leaned against the car for a minute, looking back at the building, thinking, reflecting, wondering. What if . . . ?

I would go to all the Christmas and Easter events at Our Lady of the Assumption, but that was largely because Gretchen was a student there and out of courtesy and gratitude to Sister Seraphine.

(All that was sixteen years ago, but every Christmas and Easter, I still write to Sister Seraphine and send her whatever money I can. Wouldn't you know she turns right around and gives it to charity or some deserving student.)

Gretchen was accepted into the ninth grade at another parochial school since Our Lady stopped at the eighth. The bus would pick her up, along with her friend Robin and bring them home in the afternoon. By now, she was mature enough to take care of herself, and that left me fairly free to tend to business. Though I was a confirmed workaholic, I always managed to make time for her, serving as mother, father, chauffeur, shopping assistant, cook and whatever else had to be done. It's not easy for a man to rear a daughter—questions and issues arise that no man is adequately prepared to handle. Moreover, I wondered what she was learning about God at school, but I can't recall our ever having any discussions on the matter. Maybe she thought I wasn't interested—I don't know. In any case, God remained absent from my agenda. What I did *not* know was that just because I didn't see Him or talk to Him, did not mean He wasn't there.

By this time, I had paid Al Batchelor back his ten thousand dollars in full and thanked him for having trusted in me. The spring of 1979 came, and my largest client, whom I had helped grow from a small to a large company in a very short period of time, came to me and offered me a job as head of marketing. I really didn't want to shut down my company, but on the other hand, I thought this would relieve me of a lot of pressure and allow me to spend more time with Gretchen. Those of you who own and operate your own small business know only too well how it can devour you. Collecting the money, prospecting for new business, putting out small fires that crop up daily, battling with paper work, government requirements, the list is endless. I had grown tired of it and thus I agreed to join his firm. Within a few months, it was apparent it would not work out. While he had been a client, he and I got along famously, but when I became an employee, the relationship was changed dramatically. (The company ultimately went bankrupt four years later, most of the

85

good people having left.) I had a long talk with myself and was thinking that Gretchen and I might move to Bend, Oregon, an all-but-crime-free community about which I had heard favorable reports from families who had moved there. It was evident that southern California was rapidly becoming a place that was unhealthy for children and other growing things; and I was fearful that as Gretchen moved further into adolescence, problematic at best, living here would generate pressures and temptations that I did not think would be good for her. Then quite suddenly, one Saturday morning in October, the phone rang. The familiar voice said, "Hey man, what's going on?"

Jack!

I brought him up-to-date on the events of the past year, my teaching with Drucker, my thoughts about leaving California, and when I finished he said, "Let me tell you what we're doing here at Stone." Jack gave me a thirty-minute summary of the changes that had occurred in the company and what his vision was for the future. Then he said, "Why don't you and Gretchen fly back for a quick visit, so you can get a better feel firsthand? And if you like what you see, and we can get together, I want you to be my Director of Marketing." I told him I would, we set the date for my visit, and it was not until I hung up that I realized it had been almost five years to the day since he had first called me in October of 1974 when the situation was completely reversed. At that time, *I* was the one who was in Greenville and Jack was in California, and as you have seen, it was because of *that* call I came west.

When I told Gretchen there was a good chance we might move back to Greenville, she was instantly and adamantly opposed to it. I recall our heated discussions and then her coming up with the notion that she would stay here and move in with one of her friends: "You know, Dad, they could adopt me." I told her that if I accepted the job, we would go back together, and that was that. I called both my brothers to share the news with them, and as usual, they thought I was nuts. If things were so great in California, why was I coming back to Greenville? This would always upset me, but I knew by now that no matter what I did, they would never fully understand, but that didn't matter. I knew they loved me, and that was enough.

Shortly after the conversation with Jack, Gretchen and I flew back for a whirlwind weekend, Jack made me an offer, and I accepted it on the spot. Then on Saturday, Gretchen and I went house hunting and found a lovely Cape Cod home in Forrester Woods. Gretchen fell in love with the house and her gigantic bedroom with huge closets and a bath of her own–priority one for a teenage girl. By Thanksgiving, I sold the last of my properties and we said good-bye to all our friends. Gretchen and I packed, the movers came, we put our mini poodle, Fudge, in a traveling crate and drove into the airport for the trip back. The first time I had come to Greenville, we had wound up living in a trailer park in Berea, but this time it was going to be different. I was coming back with some cash, we had a beautiful home to live in, and I had a wonderful job waiting for me.

Gretchen's anger was still smouldering within her, and I understood the reasons for this. She was leaving a place that was just now becoming a real home to her—in many ways, her first—and coming to a place where she knew no one, and for much of her life, this kind of dynamic had been the rule. Trailer to house to apartment to condominium to Greenville to Charleston to California and now back again. I hurt for her, for I remembered how fragile the world of a teenager is and how their feelings are always at flash point, their lives approaching critical mass. Yet, as a parent, I had learned that our children are far more resilient than we ever give them credit for, and I believed we would be all right.

Had we known the joy and inner peace of an authentic relationship with God then, things would have been much easier for us. Tragically, we never really talked about the subject, for it appeared that it was no more important to her than it was to me. Certainly no one could deny that good things had happened to us in California, but my upside-down logic and wrong-way theology told me that this could not have been because of God or Jesus, since I paid scant attention to the former and did not believe in the latter. All I knew was that I had the talent, guts and drive to make any situation work, and our going back to Greenville would be no different than had been my coming to California. As the plane took off from LAX, and I looked down, I thought about all the wonderful people we had known, but of all of them, it was Gail's face whom I saw for only the briefest moment and heard her words echoing in my mind:

"He has all the time in the world, and you don't. . . ."

Gretchen said, "Oh, Daddy, look."

We had broken through the clouds and the L.A. smog into a bright blue sky. I smiled at her. We were headed back to Greenville and the start of a new life.

CHAPTER
13

January 1980 found the world, as always, a study in contrasts. Mother Teresa had won the Nobel Peace Prize, but fifty Americans were in their forty-second day of being held hostages in Iran.

I paid scant attention to headlines, being caught up in my job at Stone. I spent the first several days getting acquainted with new names and faces, though many people whom I had known back in 1967 were still there. However, it was a far different company now and similarly, I was no longer the green kid who had walked in the door fourteen years earlier and talked himself into a job. Now totally computerized, they were able to keep their finger on the pulse of their markets, monitoring shipments of goods by category and customer, all this serving as a kind of early-warning system for management. Given this kind of timely and accurate data, the company now had the ability to respond to changing conditions in the market, rather than merely *react* to them. There is a world of difference between the two.

Traditionally, the apparel industry has been one of the slowest to latch on to innovation, but realizing the competitive battles that lay ahead, Jack instinctively knew that the company had to be ready to do battle in a much tougher arena than heretofore. Accordingly, he had assembled a team of tough-minded people around him who shared in his vision, and I was one of them. The camaraderie was good, we were making progress, and my work provided me with a generous measure of fulfillment and satisfaction.

Gretchen was in a private school but not at all enjoying it as I had hoped she would. Her fellow students were a bit square and slightly snobbish compared to those she had left behind in California. Among her peer group here, the symbol of admission was an alligator on a shirt or sweater, and the more of these one had, the higher one's standing rose. Everyday at school was a contest to see who would have on the latest preppy fashions. Gretchen did not buy into this, and though a good student, I'm sure her grades suffered partly as a result of her feeling out of place. She was dubbed a maverick and regarded as an outsider, and this, coupled with missing her friends in California, did not make things any easier for her. It was a difficult winter, the weather not helping at all with a seemingly endless succession of cold, grey, dismal days compared to the warm sunny ones we had known in southern California.

I sensed her unhappiness, and we talked about it, but there wasn't much I could do but keep encouraging her. I was so caught up in my new job, I'm sure I was not as attuned to her pain as I should have been. The truth was, I missed my friends from California, too, but I hoped that in our move here, she would have a better chance at growing up safe and sane. I might have deluded myself on this point, but when you're a single parent, you make the best choices you can at the time. Meanwhile, her mother had met an Englishman, adventurer type, and the two of them had gone back to London. When they would talk on the phone occasionally, Gretchen seemed to idolize the wandering, come-what-may life they led and would throw it up to me as a better alternative than the button-down tight business world in which she perceived I lived.

One night in early June—school had just ended—she had gone out for the evening with a boy who had come to the house. Things had been growing increasingly more tense between us, and I was as much to blame as she was. We would have fights that were shouting matches, but words can hurt worse than blows. Unfortunately, this was all I knew how to do. I demanded the truth from her in all things, and that was the problem. I did not know then that truth without compassion and love is intellectual arrogance, perhaps the most deadly and destructive form of pride. Fearing my disapproval and rejection, and the violent tirades that I would launch into, Gretchen was too frightened to be open with me. Add to that my own insecurity, and it was like pouring gasoline on a fire. She would say she'd be happier off living with her mother, and that would ignite my temper. I didn't want her going back to that kind of life, and the fact that she would choose that over her life here only angered me further. I could only see things in terms of how ungrateful she was. After all, wasn't I providing her with a good home, a good education and so on. (We've all had that said to us, haven't we—or said it to someone else.) The problem was, I was as far from the truth as she was, but couldn't admit it.

Worse still was the stress from work, magnified by my own fierce desire to excel. I was a strict disciplinarian, as my mother had been with us. Love was something you gave or received, based upon a sliding scale of what you might expect to get back for it. It was a tool, a device, a test that you took in the hopes of making a good grade in life. I did not know about *God's* love for us as manifested through Christ. In any event, I awoke at some time after midnight, the time she was due home, and checked her room to make sure she was there. Finding her bed empty, I began to worry a bit but not unduly. Surely, she would be in before long. I could not get to sleep and lay there waiting for the sound of the key in the lock. Finally, at about four-thirty, I heard the door open, and I heard her go into her bathroom. After a minute or so, I arose and walked down the hall. The door was open and she was standing there gazing at herself in the mirror with a strange kind of look, as though she were trying to determine who the person was in the mirror looking back at her. Drugs? Sex? Beer? All of the above? I didn't know.

"Oh, hi, Dad," she said. "I just got up to use the bathroom."

"When did you get home?"

"About one. I'm sorry I was late."

I told her that was all right and to go on to bed. I went back to my room and by now was seething with anger, and I lay there, hearing her go to bed. When I could stand it no longer, I sat up in bed, clicked on my light and reached for the phone. I had made a decision. Promptly at seven in the morning—she had had no more than two hours sleep—I woke her and told her to get up and get dressed right now. Blinking the sleep from her eyes, she wanted to know why.

"If nothing else, I deserve the truth from you, Gretchen. I know you got home at 4:30. I was up all night worrying about you, don't you know that? If there's no truth between us, then we don't have anything to build on, and it doesn't seem like you want to deal with that. You've been telling me all along that you'd be happier living with your mother. Well, that's exactly where you're going!" The words came out in a snarl. I don't believe she had ever seen me this angry, and that was sufficient motivation for her to leap out of bed and get packed. We wolfed down a quick breakfast without looking at one another, then climbed in the car and two-and-a-half tense and wordless hours later, we were standing at the BOAC loading gate at the Atlanta airport. She had a one-way ticket in her hand for London, her mother knew she was coming, and that was it. Now as the agent announced the boarding, she stood there in line with the ticket. I gave her a perfunctory hug, but it was one statue holding another.

"G'bye, Dad," she said. "I love you."

"I love you too, Gretchen," and then she disappeared into the boarding gate. I stood there for a moment, then turned on my heel, walked through the endless airport, found my car, drove the 150 miles back to Greenville, turned into Forrester Woods, pulled into the garage, went upstairs and into my bathroom then fell on my knees and threw up in the toilet.

The rest of the day I spent crying. I had never been more lonely or frightened in my life. If only those tears could have come earlier, they might have washed away the wall that my pride and her fear had erected between us. Moreover, I found myself wondering if Gretchen had been right, after all. Maybe we should have stayed in California. And while I wondered, I wept.

Summer came in earnest, bringing with it the humidity that I had forgotten all about while living in California. The house seemed twice as large as it actually was. I would roam around, finally open the door to her bedroom and look in, then close it and

92

turn my thoughts to other matters. I wrote Gretchen in London, but did not hear a word in return. I kept on writing. Finally, after about a month, I received a letter from her. She said she was working hard cleaning bathrooms with her mom in fish and chips houses and doing whatever the three of them could do to get by. There was anger in her voice, but I had expected that. I deserved it. She had to get it out of her, and equally important, I needed to hear it. To wrestle with it. To accept it. I read it over and over, then tucked it into one of the cubby holes in my rolltop desk.

By the time fall came, there were a half dozen or so of these letters in the cubby, each one revealing the progressive growth that Gretchen was experiencing, and I read them, my heart continued to soften, and I knew that I loved her more than ever. Then one morning in late October, she called and said she wanted to come home. I told her that was wonderful news, and I would wire the money for the ticket. She arrived home on Halloween day, enrolled at Mauldin High and we resumed our lives together. Neither of us was the person we had been when she left. She had seen a side of life she had not known before, and I had had time to understand how deep my love was for her and my need for her as well as her need for me.

We both wrote a contract, she putting down what she expected from me, and vice versa. We signed it, then tacked it up on our bedroom doors. (This may sound unusual, but I strongly recommend this for parents and teenagers and will have more to say about the logic behind this later.)

It was not until mid-winter that an opportunity presented itself for me to put my love for her and belief *in* her into action and give it wings. I had come home from work later than usual and noticed the door to her room closed. I knocked on it and asked if she was all right, and her response was a muffled but tearful yes. I asked permission to come in—I always did that—and when I entered, I found Gretchen seated on the floor by her bed. It was obvious she had been crying, and I anticipated the worst, but before I could ask any questions, she thrust something into my hand. It was a presentation folder filled with a dozen or so pages, and she explained that their English teacher had assigned them a creative project, and Gretchen had chosen to write about what her own birth must have been like. She said they could use original art, drawings, poetry, clippings: whatever they felt was necessary to make the story real.

"Daddy, you've been a teacher. I want you to read this and see what grade you would have given me. Don't read what she wrote until you finish it."

I took it into my room and read it, being as objective as a father can possibly be, and decided it was definitely not "A" material, but deserved a good, solid B. Then I read what the teacher had written: something to the effect that it was overly erotic, obscene and in bad taste. Grade? D minus. I was stunned. I thumbed through it again to make sure I hadn't missed anything. Then I started to simmer, and before long, the simmer had turned into a racing boil. I went back to Gretchen's room and asked for the name of her counselor. She told me her name was Janet Sweat and that she was a wonderful person, in her early thirties, black, married, very understanding, but overworked with too great a case load. I think there were three counselors for a school of 700 students. The next day I called Janet and we had a long talk about Gretchen, the teacher and the project. I told her that I wanted to come talk to her and the teacher, who was a practice teacher, as soon as possible. She set it up for the following morning, and at nine o'clock, Gretchen, the teacher, "Miss Tompkins," Janet and I met in Janet's office, a small glass windowed office just off the library.

Miss Tompkins came in after Janet introduced us, we sat down. She was in her early twenties, dressed very conservatively with a long skirt, her hair done in a severe style. Janet explained that I had called for the meeting and then said, "Mr. Levin has a few things to say to you."

"Miss Tompkins," I began. "I—"

"Please, call me Sarah," she said, managing a slight smile.

"I'd be glad too. Sarah, before we talk about Gretchen or the project, I'd like to tell you a little bit about my background, since it may help. I have a B.A. in English from the University of North Carolina where I graduated Phi Beta Kappa, and I earned my

94

master's degree from the University of Iowa. I've taught ninth and eleventh grades, college and graduate school, both in English language and literature, business communications and creative writing. My students have ranged from those coming from mill backgrounds over at Spartanburg Methodist to adults in an MBA sequence."

I paused, watching her. The pleasant smile was frozen in place.

"I've also written and published a few stories, poems and the like." I looked up at her. She ran her tongue over her upper lip, her eyes unblinking. Janet cleared her throat. Gretchen sat motionless.

"When Gretchen showed me her project, she was in tears, and I have never before seen her so upset over her school work. She asked me to take a look at it, and I did. I read through it very carefully, and though I disagree with the grade it received, that's not the real issue, so let me get beyond that. Sarah, my real concern is about your comments—about its being erotic and obscene." I waited. Her face was a mask.

"So, with that in mind, I'd like to read something to you, if that's okay." She gave me a slight smile and nodded.

I opened a binder I had been holding in my lap and began to read:

"How graceful are your feet in sandals, O queenly maiden! Your rounded thighs are like jewels, the work of a master hand. Your navel is a rounded bowl that never lacks mixed wine. Your belly is a heap of wheat, encircled with lilies. Your two breasts are like two fawns, twins of a gazelle. . . . How fair and pleasant you are, O loved one, delectable maiden! You are stately as a palm tree, and your breasts are like its clusters. I say I will climb the palm tree and lay hold of its branches. Oh, may your breasts be like clusters of the vine, and the scent of your breath like apples, and your kisses like the best wine that goes down smoothly, gliding over lips and teeth."

95

Well before I finished reading, she began to blush a deep crimson and looked down at her hands that were clutched tightly in her lap.

"Now I would say that's fairly erotic, wouldn't you? In fact, it's probably some of the most erotic literature I know of and yet, handled so beautifully and with such sensitivity, too."

"It's The Song of Solomon," she said in a tiny voice.

I nodded. "You know, Solomon was able to work this kind of magic. But Gretchen, being barely fifteen and a rank beginner—well, it's altogether different. All art tries to portray the world as seen through the eyes of the artist, and that's what Gretchen was trying to do. Granted, the attempt was somewhat clumsy and a bit naive, but consider the writer and the age. Having been a teacher, the toughest lesson I had to learn was to separate myself from my feelings in grading my students. In fact, in several cases, some of the students I liked the least wound up getting the highest grades from me." I paused then turned in my chair so I was facing her head on. "Now what I am asking you to do is this: in light of what we've discussed, I would consider it a great help to her if you would review her project and regrade it. Whatever you come up with, we'll accept."

I waited. She gave no indication she was ready to budge an inch. I didn't want to do what I was about to do next, but she left me no choice.

"Sarah, I understand your position; now I want you to understand mine. My work calls for me to maintain a close working relationship with regional and national media, both print and the electronic. And if you decide *not* to regrade it, within forty-eight hours this story and your name and this school will show up on every major wire service in the country, and for one reason. What you did was not only unfair, it was unprofessional, and though I'm sure you didn't mean to, you hurt my daughter and as her father, I am committed to come to her defense."

She sat there as though glued to the chair. Janet seemed to have turned a different shade than her lovely mahogany hue. Gretchen's eyes seemed to grow larger. Sarah began speaking in a whisper.

"I . . . you must understand, I was reared in a very strict religious home, and I didn't . . . I don't know much about the way the world is. I was educated in a fundamentalist school, and I realize I have a lot of things to work on before I can be a fair teacher and . . . this is one of them. It's just that this kind of thing has always been so difficult for me, even to talk about. But yes: I *will* re-grade her project."

Then she turned to Gretchen.

"Gretchen . . . I'm sorry for hurting you."

Janet asked Gretchen to leave the room and wait outside in the library then turned to me and said, "Mr. Levin, I'm glad we have been able to work this out quietly and to the satisfaction of everyone. Sarah, I won't keep you anymore, as I know you have a class waiting."

Miss Tompkins walked out. I thanked Janet for her help then walked out into the library. Gretchen was waiting there for me, hollered out "Daddy," and literally flew through the air at me, attaching herself to me, with all arms and legs. From that day on, we were and have remained father and daughter. We both realized we didn't need a written contract anymore, took it down and tossed it and celebrated by going out to eat Chinese, her favorite.

She still knew that I would go up against her when I thought she was in the wrong. But that I would fight for her when she was in the right.

We have not violated that contract to this day.

CHAPTER
14

I remained at Stone for three years, finding new challenges in everything that came along. Jack, always the marketeer, kept seeking new markets and opportunities. Some panned out, some didn't, but you only have to make one big strike, and that makes up for all the rest. He was fascinated by the growing interest in soccer among young people. Of course, as America entered the 80's, soccer was fighting for a toehold and was not even recognized by many schools. Indeed, most high schools would begrudge players a field and facilities, with the result that private teams or neighborhood "clubs" sprang up with the support of parents. Then Jack heard about a man traveling around New England selling Umbro soccer wear literally out of the trunk of his car. He had gotten the rights from the parent company in England to sell Umbro in the U.S. Jack and he met, became acquainted, Stone bought the company, and all the rest is history. Today Umbro is one of the leading brands of soccer wear and equipment not only here at home but around the world as well, and Stone owns the copyright worldwide.

By the end of '82, the old restlessness came over me. I had made the important contributions to the company's forward momentum by helping to reposition themselves in this new market, and I was ready to move on, with Jack's blessing. It was time to start my own company once more. I was going to say "be my own boss," but let us please not delude ourselves. We are never our own bosses, for whether we head up a hole-in-the-wall hand laundry or a billion-dollar conglomerate, ultimately we answer to *someone*, first on earth, in the form of our customers who can make or break us. Next, we answer to our bodies, to the abuse of neglect or the slow, silent creep of time; we answer to the wrong doing of others that can cancel our ticket at any time; and we remain vulnerable to a host of other earthbound, mortal afflictions and events that can descend upon us like a plague of locusts.

Finally, and most importantly, we are answerable to God. Count on it.

I had sold our home in the fall of '82 and bought a small condominium that would be easier to maintain. Six months later in March, I found a small office to rent , and hung out my shingle and reactivated The Bottom Line, Inc. By now, Gretchen was in college and naturally very concerned whether she would have to drop out because of my going out on my own. I told her not to worry, we'd find a way. Sure enough, I found a job playing piano on weekends in The Fish Market, an upscale restaurant; and every Friday and Saturday nights after I finished work, I would run home, shower, change into formal wear, and play from seven until midnight. I received sixty dollars in cash for the two nights, and after being paid at midnight on Saturday, I would walk across the parking lot to The Family Mart and buy our groceries for the coming week, then drive home and fall into bed exhausted.

We made the mortgage payment, had food on the table, and luckily, Gretchen had urged me to apply for scholarship assistance. I did and help came through. Otherwise, she might have had to drop out of school. She was fast becoming a very sensible, practical person and was learning how to cope with the roadblocks that life has a tendency to erect in our path.

I began my business with no clients—as usual. But if you demonstrate an authentic desire to help people, along with the proven ability to do the work, business will come to you. People will seek you out because these commodities have always been in short supply in the business arena and are becoming increasingly so. Thus one by one, clients came aboard. A project here, an assignment there, and TBL, as it came to be known, began to grow. By the end of the year, there were three of us, and we moved to larger space. Truth to tell, we were just paying the bills,

100

and I took what little money was left over for Gretchen and I to live on. My reputation was good in the marketplace, but small agencies have a tough time acquiring large clients, thus you go from project to project, and to keep up with the crunch, I was working eighty hours a week. I needed a break, and just as in the past, it came when I least expected it and in the most unusual manner.

It was a cold Saturday morning in March. The day had dawned with a hard, driving rain keeping people indoors for the most part. But Saturday was like any other day for me, and I had taken a break from work to do some errands and on the way back, decided to swing by a sandwich place and pick up some lunch to take back to the office. As I ducked inside, I bumped into someone who was leaving, and though it had been twelve years or more since I last saw him, I remembered him.

"Ward Stone, how are you?" I proffered my hand, and he looked at me but couldn't put my face with a name. (Ward was Gene Stone's brother and had worked at the company for years before leaving to pursue private interests.) I refreshed his memory, and we stood there chatting for a moment, though he was in a hurry to leave. Then, and for whatever reason I might have had, I asked him about Bill Wise, who had been sales manager at Stone and had then gone on to head up Wrangler for Boys. Ward said that as best he knew, Bill was now the president of Stedman. He pumped my hand, picked up his sandwiches and dashed out the door and into his car.

I went back to the office and gave that some serious thought. Bill had befriended me during the year I was at Stone, back in the mid-sixties, and I had always found him to be an engaging and genuine fellow. Even after I left the company the first time, we had kept in touch, and he had taken a genuine interest in my progress and would call me from time to time when our name would crop up in the media. Stedman was a large apparel firm headquartered in Asheboro, North Carolina, and though I didn't know very much about them, I decided I would write Bill a long letter bringing him up-to-date.

Bill responded with a phone call, told me what was happen-

101

ing there, and before I knew it, he and his Director of Marketing, Mick Murtha, drove down to Greenville to visit us in our offices which could be best described as "early american humble." We did have indoor plumbing, but after that, it fell off rapidly. Mick seemed to take no notice, and the upshot was that after an intense and probing conversation, he said he wanted us to be Stedman's agency. It was like the incident with Dr. Brigham and Snowshoe, all over again. Our little company was only three people: a secretary, an art director and me, but that didn't matter to Mick. He and I clicked from the moment we met, and today, some ten years later, we are still the closest of friends. It has been that way with nearly all my clients over the years, just as it had been with my father and his customers.

Now, when you are in advertising and marketing, and you acquire a new client—especially one who has an urgent, real need and the resources to match—it is very close to falling in love when you are young. The heart beats faster, and you can barely contain yourself because of the excitement. The first thing you do is get on the phone and call everyone you know to tell them the news, and it takes a week or more to come back down to earth. Media people and suppliers flock around you hoping to get some of the gravy, and you bask in that for a while. It's all ego, of course, even though agencies would deny this and insist the reason for their being excited about new clients is that they want to help the company fulfill its marketing goals. I don't deny that, but it would be closer to the truth to say a new client brings the thrill of more work, more money and a great boost for the ego in terms of awards and strokes from their peer group. It's a shot of adrenalin for an agency, and whether agency folk say it openly or otherwise to their competitors, the words are on their lips: *eat your heart out!*

Stedman allowed us to shift into overdrive, and though the work load was terribly exciting, it was also crushing. I looked for another person to help, but you simply do not run out and hire good people overnight. There was barely time to respond to the demands: a new image, a new thrust, new product entries, and all of it had to be done yesterday. Of course, hearing that is like the sound of the alarm to a firehouse dog, and you are ready to run flat out at a moment's notice. Being given this opportunity gave us the chance to expand and grow, and a year later, I bought a house on Mills Avenue that became both office for TBL and home for Gretchen and myself.

Our business grew apace, though in less than a year, there was a management change at Stedman, with Mick and Bill leaving, which led in turn to our resigning the account. However, by now we had gained sufficient momentum and exposure so that clients began coming to us of their own accord. Gretchen graduated college and married a man she had met years before in high school and with whom she had maintained an on-again, off-again relationship. I barely knew him, but gave the marriage my blessing and got behind it solidly. That's a parent's job.

Of course, it wasn't as though I didn't have my own hands full with the business. We were running around the oval on the Indy 500, where on any given day there would be enough high octane pumping in our arteries to blow an engine, but we managed to keep our cool and stay together. I had a key person, Tricia Trent, who did the work of two ordinary people, and with her in place, we had one more vital position to fill—that of art director.

I had gone through several of these but needed someone who could mesh with me and run at my pace. Though I was wired for 220, most other people were wired for 110—normal household current. Consequently, and without intending to, in demanding the best from them, the downside was that I tended to burn them out, and this led to disappointment and regret for all. Not a very healthy situation on which to build relationships, but I didn't know any differently. I ran an ad and a few people applied, and then late Friday afternoon, a young woman called to inquire about the position. Her name was Deborah Dayhoff, and after we said our introductions, I fired a broadside at her.

"What took you so long? The ad ran four days ago."

"I know," she said, "but someone just showed it to me. I really want to work with you. Please. At least, talk with me." There was a breathless quality to her voice, a genuine eagerness

103

that caught my interest, and I decided it was worthwhile to keep listening. The first thing she told me about herself was that she was a Christian: a graduate of Bob Jones University. (BJU is an excellent Christian school with a strongly fundamentalist theology which unfortunately has led to its being looked upon askance, unfairly so, by many Greenvillians.) Deborah's husband was in seminary there, and I asked her what was she doing now.

"Selling for a sign company, on commission."

For an ad agency, sign people are lumped in with used car salesmen, but I was so taken with her enthusiasm and conviction that I told her to come over, bring her portfolio, and we'd talk. She showed up in twenty minutes, glowing with excitement. We talked for an hour or more downstairs in my working room or "think tank." Deb could not only draw and design but was also a whiz on the then state-of-the-art typesetting equipment in addition to being a marvelous calligrapher. Her candor and high energy were in sync with mine, and I began to feel better and better about her.

She knew I was Jewish, and I said to her jokingly, just don't try to convert me. She blushed at this, then gave me a smile. I told her that I'd try to watch my language when I was around her, but that I could rant and rave, drink, go on a rampage if something was not done right, but she seemed to accept this with aplomb. I suppose I was trying to scare her off, but I was to learn that Deb does not frighten that easily. I showed her some of the work we had done, and this excited her all the more. Finally, I offered her the job, and Monday morning, she showed up for work raring to go.

Deb's entrance into my life and the life of the agency signaled a major turning point. In retrospect, neither of us could have known the full import of this, just as I did not know what impact Gail Ressel would have on my life nearly a decade earlier. I had also hired a high school junior earlier in the year, Wendy Donald, who ran errands for us, but one day when she told us she had to quit because of commitments at school, she sent over her mother, Trish, to sub for her. Trish was a warm Christian angel:

104

black, mother of three, who would sing gospel hymns to herself while she would fix my lunch. So along with Trish, there we were: Tricia, a devout Catholic; Deb, a vibrant Christian; and me, the wild and crazy Jew on the road to fame and glory. The chemistry was volatile at times, and we had our share of flare-ups and explosions, but somehow it worked. The reason for this could be summed up in one word: *grace*. Of course, I had no idea then what that meant. I thought "grace" was what you said at mealtime. (Dear reader, please do not ponder how someone could be so ignorant of the kingdom of God. So out of touch with the Creator. It happened then. It happens now. Just take a look around.)

As I write these lines, I look at a framed work of calligraphy sitting in front of me, beautifully executed and handsomely mounted. On it are these verses:

> *O Lord, Thou has searched me and known me.*
> *Even before there is a word on my tongue,*
> *Behold, O Lord, Thou dost know it all.*

At the bottom in very small lettering or what she and I used to refer to as "mouse" type was this inscription: To Ron from Deb Dayhoff. Christmas 1985. Psalm 139:1-4.

When she gave it to me the night of our Christmas party, I was very touched by the gesture and moved by its beauty. When everyone had gone home, I hung it on the wall in my bedroom and from time to time I would glance at it but with no lingering interest.

Deb and I, along with the rest of the team, started to generate work that was second to none. Clients would come to visit us, feel our energy, I would take them down in the think tank for a whirlwind, eye-opening session, with me standing at the easel, laying out the core of a strategic plan right before their eyes—without giving away the store, of course—and tell them things about their company and their competitors they didn't even know. Their eyes would widen, their fingers drum the table in anticipation, and then at the precise moment, Trish Donald would come downstairs and serve a lunch that was absolutely scrumptious. People felt right at home at TBL and they knew the commitment was genuine, and that we would treat them fairly. Deb's mere presence served as a kind of moral reminder for me, though this did not stop me from pouring my generous jolt of Jack Daniels at day's end and drinking it before her. Her cute little nose would wrinkle at the sour mash smell, coupled with an almost imperceptible rise of her eyebrows, signaling tacit disapproval, but I did it anyway because . . . well, that's the way I was. Jack Black and I had more than a nodding acquaintance, though I managed to keep it in check—or thought I did.

Deb and I would sit and have long conversations about her faith, her family, her dreams. When Allan, her husband, finished seminary, they would go somewhere and plant a church.

"Where is somewhere?" I asked her one day.

"Wherever the Lord leads us," she said, giving me that wonderful look that made you feel as though you were two years old.

"You mean, you don't know. Right?"

"Ron," she said, "the Lord will take care of us when the time comes. It's not given to us to know at this time."

"And you're going to go away and leave me?"

"You got it."

I would put on a stage face of fear, fright, dismay and tears, and that would make her laugh. We could do that. Deb and I even had names for each other. For her, I was Ronbo, lacking only the bandoliers and the assault rifle that the real life Rambo carried. For me, she was Harley Dayhoff, for all I had to do was give her an idea, and she'd be off like a motorcycle racing light to light. Yet, her seemingly boundless energy and talent, coupled with a childlike innocence, was undergirded by a quiet, resolute faith, the latter clearly evident in her every action and word. The same with Trish Donald, but a bit more vocal, for Trish's heart sang and leapt like a gospel hymn sung by Aretha. However, after an initial squaring off and recognizing each other's gifts and graces, the two of them, along with Tricia Trent, came to be warm, close friends and served as my guardian angels.

106

As strange as it may sound, others came to work for us part time from Bob Jones, and I would often think to myself, we were becoming a Bob Jones off-campus satellite, owned by the third son of a Russian Jew. Go figure! What I didn't know was that God had a very definite reason for sending all these Christians to me, just as He had with Jack Stone, Jason and Lisa, Gail Ressel, Al Batchelor and so many others, but had you told me this I would have poured myself another two fingers of Jack Black and had a good laugh.

All the seemingly disparate pieces fit wonderfully together and generated an incredible synergy that suppliers, clients and yes, even competitors, marveled at. I didn't profess to understand it myself. No matter. I had bought my ticket for the roller coaster, and I was going to sit back, hold on and enjoy the ride.

CHAPTER
15

$\mathbf{G}$retchen came to me one afternoon and said she needed to talk. I sat there while she told me that her marriage was all but over, and she was going to get a divorce. The pain in her face was all too apparent. Trish Donald had predicted it months before, having served almost as a surrogate mother to Gretchen, but I had resolved to wait until I heard it straight from my daughter's lips. Meanwhile, I had made a conscious effort not to interfere, and now I told Gretchen that I would help in any way that I could and that I was there for her. That commitment, plus a hug, was what she needed from me, and she left to work out the details on her own. When she had gone, I sat there lost in thought. I was relieved that she was going to dissolve the marriage, for even though I had given them my love and help, I had ached for her from the start.

We may be human, but in one respect, we're like bluebirds or bears, since our job in parenting is to prepare our children to *leave* us, not to stay. And ever since she had come to live with me, I had encouraged her independence so that she might grow up strong, yet resilient and possessing a set of values that would sustain her. There were rules, yes, and as I have mentioned, we had a contract in which our obligations to the other were set forth, but that's the way it *ought* to be with parents and children. That way, no one can come back later—as so frequently happens today in this country–and claim that "we never agreed to that," or "I didn't promise that," or "when did I say *that*?"

Baloney!

Put it down in writing and live by it, until after a while, it's written on your heart. Then, as we did, throw away the piece of paper and get a life. The mother bear has to teach her cubs not to mess with porcupines, skunks or avoid getting too near the edge of the cliff. We have to do the same, but we have to be careful that in the doing, we don't kill the spirit within them, for that is the most valuable legacy we can leave to them.

A word about those letters she had written from England. When she graduated Furman, I gave them to her, and though she never talked about them, I'm sure she read them over and over, seeing the girl she had once been and the woman she was now. Whatever happened, Gretchen knew I would be there for her, and I knew that she would emerge from the experience stronger and wiser. As the watchful momma/poppa, I resolved to keep a sharp eye out in case it got a little explosive, which it ultimately did. But the divorce was finally granted, she got rid of the house and began her new life.

Back to business.

One day, a client of mine and friend, Howard Suitt, called me and asked if I'd consider conducting a "strategic marketing" seminar for his company down at Myrtle Beach. Suitt Construction had carved out a rather enviable niche in the construction business in the Southeast, and we had been doing various things for them over the years. Actually, they had been a client of mine when I left to go to California in 1974, and when I had hung out my shingle again, nine years later, they became a client for the second time.

Howard had decided to assemble his management and sales team for a two-day session, and he wanted me to have them on the opening morning, from ten to twelve. I agreed, not exactly knowing what I was going to do, but the more I thought about it, and based upon my comprehensive knowledge of the company's operations, I put together something that I thought would focus their attention on what was important. I used some famous win/lose stories from the marketplace, glued it together with some old tricks and stuff from my Bowery days, found some neat props, gleaned some workable wisdom and tactics that had worked for other companies, and I figured this might help them to take a fresh new look at the way they had been doing things in the past. I didn't even know the word, then, but what I was really doing

110

was helping them to break out of their paradigm.

The morning came with fifteen people assembled in a conference room, and I let 'em have it with both barrels. It was a blend of shock theater, SWAT team and scrimmage without helmets on. There were laughs, frowns, grins and grunts galore. I put people on the spot and then got them out of it by having them laugh at themselves. I got them to challenge old ways of looking at things. I led them to talk openly about things that had been taboo for discussion and broke down whatever barriers or pre-conceived notions they might have brought into the room.

Suddenly, Howard said, "Ron, I know everybody is enjoying this, but I really think we need to bring this to a close. We're running into our tee-time."

I glanced at my watch and realized I had been on for nearly two-and-a-half hours, nonstop. No one had noticed until now. The team broke for a quick box lunch, then headed for the golf course, and I stayed to chat with one of the board members who had flown in from out west. While munching his sandwich, he eyed me for a moment or two then said, "I guess you stay pretty booked up, don't you?"

I didn't get it, and the puzzled look on my face told him as much.

"You know . . . doing these seminars. Ron, this was really great! Just what Suitt needed."

I said, "Well, actually, I don't do this as a business or anything. I just did this one as a kind of favor for Howard, you know, their being a client and all."

"A favor!" He put down his sandwich and looked directly at me. "Listen, Ron, I've been to things like this all over the country. I've seen them all, and I'm telling you, what you did this morning would rank up there with the best of them."

The tone in this voice told me he was deadly serious and not trying to stroke my ego. This man didn't have to. He looked around. Howard had left the room to join the guys on the course. "Say, if you don't mind my asking, what did you charge Howard for this?"

"Five hundred."

His mouth opened in amazement. "Five hun . . . do you realize you could charge five times that or more for what you did and companies would pay for it gladly?"

I shook my head.

"Well, my friend, you think about it. I think you're crazy if you don't pursue this. The best part is: unlike what you're doing now, you don't have to hang around and hold their hands. You do it, eat the rubber chicken, pick up the check and head home. Know what I mean?" He gave me a knowing look, and I nodded in assent.

The drive back to Greenville from Myrtle Beach is endless, and being a weekday, off-season, the traffic was light. As I drove, I thought about what he had said. By the time I passed through Columbia, a picture was beginning to form in my mind. I knew that the challenge was in the packaging. A seminar is a product just like any other product, and the first thing you learn about a new product is that it has to have a name that positions it in the marketplace: in other words, sets it apart from the others on the shelf. Better still, the name should say what it does but in a way that is attention-getting and memorable. *Mop'n Glo, Endust, Carefree, I Can't Believe It's Not Butter, Weight Watchers*— just walk through your supermarket and see for yourself. For that reason, I knew that if I called it something bland like Marketing Workshop or Strategic Planning Seminar, it would sound just like all the others: too dull and deadly academic.

I thought about what had captured the attention of the group, and I began to lay those ideas side by side in my mind, and then one central thought brought it together. The group had liked it the most when I made things tough on them—making them feel as if they didn't know anything—and that made them laugh at each other even while they were learning some hard lessons . . . almost like recruits in boot camp.

Boot camp . . . *yesss!*

I would call it: *Boot Camp for Marketeers.*

By the time I pulled into my garage, I had it all put together. The first thing to do was develop what we call a broadside: you get them all the time, from the very fancy ones for Publisher's

112

Clearing House all the way down to offers from record companies, insurance, flower bulbs, magazine subscriptions, whatever. Of course, I didn't have tens of thousands of dollars to spend on fancy photography and lush, four-color printing, and I couldn't afford to wait six months until it was done.

Working day and night, I and my staff created a hard hitting, high impact piece that I hoped would do the job. As it was being printed, I ordered a mailing list of the major trade and industry associations in the Carolina's, figuring that would be the easiest place to get a toehold in the market and gain some exposure. The list came in, the broadside was ready, I added a personal letter with a reply card and sent it out, then waited.

The first call came from a farm equipment dealer's association. We talked, he wanted to know the amount of my fee to do an hour, and I took a deep breath and said, "Seven fifty."

"Plus travel and lodging, of course," he said.

"Oh, of course." I held my breath.

"That sounds just fine. I'll send you a letter of confirmation."

Okay, now get the picture: I show up at this posh resort, all stoked and ready to go, and just before I'm introduced, the president asks the widow of a recently deceased former association president to stand up and say a few words. She starts reminiscing, bursts into tears, and soon the whole room is sniffing and honking along with her. By the time she sits down, there is not a dry eye in the house, and then the presenter clears his throat, and says, "And now, how about giving a warm welcome to our next speaker, Ron Levin."

It was a wake without a funeral. Everything was wrong. I was sandwiched behind a podium and I couldn't mingle with the audience who were seated below me. I did the best I could, but it was like speaking at an undertaker's convention. I couldn't start off with anything funny or shocking or dramatic, so I had to transition into my bit very gently, and that took some doing. When it was over, the applause was good, but I was far from satisfied. Of course, they always pay you, no matter how bad you think you may have done, but what surprised me is that the people loved it, but I gave myself a 3 on a scale of 10. On the long trip back, I did a post mortem and figured out what I could have done and *should* have done. I was always my severest critic, but that's what you have to do when you're plowing new ground and don't have anyone to guide you.

Three weeks passed, and one morning I received a call from the American Furniture Manufacturer's Association. They were having a national meeting of marketing people in Charlotte and wanted me to do an hour and a half as the meeting wrap-up. I took another deep breath and told her $1,250. That was fine. I requested and received all the intelligence and information I could get so I would be fully armed and knowledgeable about the industry: problems, past history, current situation, winners, losers, macro-economic forces affecting the marketplace, trends— the whole nine yards. I had learned over the years to process this kind of data and from it, synthesize a set of strategies and solutions that might let some daylight in.

The room was huge, packed with movers and shakers from dozens of major furniture manufacturers. I came on and did an hour, and things were really going strong, when the mike went out, but I leapt on top of a table and finished the last twenty minutes without it, and when I wound up, the entire audience was on their feet applauding, cheering and whistling. Then an elderly man came forward, and the room became hushed. He took hold of me and said, "I've been coming to these things for forty years, and I learned more about this business from you than I could have ever imagined." Everybody stood up and applauded again. Then he introduced himself to me as Nat Ancell. That didn't mean anything to me, but a few minutes later the president of the association drew me aside, and said, "Ron, you don't know who Nathan is, do you?" I shook my head.

"I didn't think so. He's a legend in the industry, and someone whom we revere and admire more than anyone else. Nat is the founding genius behind Ethan Allen."

After that, doors started to open and the word got out. GTE, Alcoa, Panasonic, Milliken, Mobile Instruments, major banks— this group, that association. I appeared at DisneyWorld twice, on the program with Art Linkletter and later with Louise Mandrell,

114

and it was sheer delight. By now I had outfitted myself in uniform and would come on in army fatigues with a footlocker of props that ranged from dummy grenades, smoke bombs, a gas mask—whatever I could use to dramatize and drive home a point. People loved it and as time passed, I was finally getting $3,000 to $3,500 for an hour and a half. Of course, there was some preparation time involved, for I had to do my homework, but this was awfully big money for me. At first I felt guilty taking it, but companies paid it gladly, and they said I was worth it. Some said I was worth more. Hey, Mom, look at me go! *Vrooom!*

The irony here is that all I did was to take what I had learned thirty years earlier in The Bowery, plus what I learned from business and teaching and life and wrap it up into one package and people loved it. More important, it had real impact on companies, because I could tell from the feedback I received following the events. With the additional money, I bought the house next door and fixed it up to be rented out as an office. The business had moved into yet another building on the corner since we needed more growing room. Deb's husband, Allan, graduated seminary, and they moved to Virginia to plant a church. Trish Donald wanted to graduate to a "serious" job at the newspaper, and with their absence, a gradual yet tangible change began to take place in the business. Looking back at this, I can only tell you that things were not the same.

I know now what it was—I and the others had experienced a death of the spirit, and with Deb and Trish gone, and their spiritual presence no longer there, it was an open invitation for Satan to walk in the back door. Regrettably, I never noticed, being too busy keeping up with the business walking in the front door. The Bottom Line was flourishing. My work had been published in leading textbooks, and clients continued to come to us. I moved the business into larger headquarters and got my house back to live in. Gretchen had resolved her divorce on her own and had emerged from it stronger and with a higher degree of self-esteem. She was like her old self, and yet with a new level of confidence and stability, and that delighted me.

115

Something else happened that I must have shoved back into my unconscious and forgotten about, because it just came to me in doing the final editing of the book. In the spring of '89, I was coming back from visiting a client in Texas, a loveable, tough-minded but tenderhearted character named "Brink" Brinkman, and I had to change planes in Atlanta and catch a commuter—a puddle jumper—on into Greenville. It was a Saturday and there were about fifteen of us–a small group–waiting to board, and we were already twenty minutes behind time. Finally, the agent comes over and says that our plane was being checked over by the mechanics, and that we would be boarding shortly. Another twenty minutes passed, and he told us to move up to the next gate where a new plane had been readied for us, and we would board immediately. As we picked up our things, I noticed that the sign where we *had* been standing had been changed from Greenville to Macon, meaning the plane we had been scheduled to take–the one they were working on–would be the one that would fly to Macon, that is, once it was fixed.

While watching the eleven o'clock news that night, I happened to catch the tail end of a piece about a commuter plane having crashed that afternoon out of Atlanta. I stayed up and waited for CNN, and at midnight, they had the details on. It had been the flight for Macon and was the same commuter plane, same airline. It had to have been the plane we would have boarded for Greenville. I poured myself two fingers of Jack Black and sat there for a long while nursing my drink . . . and thinking. Oddly enough, this wasn't something I felt like talking about, so I kept it to myself.

Now I have to tell you "a story within a story." About an event that happened that at the time did not seem like anything extraordinary, but oh, when God wants to engineer His plan and it starts to come together, look out. Just listen to this impossible script:

During Christmas, Gretchen goes home to visit her mother in Charleston. Sally lines her up a blind date. Gretchen falls in love. She and this young man come back to Greenville and decide to

116

live together. I see that she is happy, so I am not concerned at this point. Frankly, after the unhappiness she had known, I would much rather have her live in a non-married relationship where she is happy and loved than in a marriage where she is miserable and threatened.

The man was a topnotch, quality-minded contractor-painter-builder who set up his own business. Two years passed and Gretchen became aware that the relationship had changed for the worse, the man having done a chameleon change into something else than he purported to be. She knew she needed to get out of it. As always, I told her I was there for her if she needed me. She was old enough now to handle these things on her own, having gained the strength from her previous experiences. Plus, I had enough to worry about. With the recession, I had down-sized the business, as the first thing companies cut in a recession is the advertising budget. Additionally, they put a hold on expensive seminars, conventions, sales meetings and the like. We were managing to pay the bills and salaries, but that was about it. In the process, we lost some good people, hired others, but the chemistry was not right. Our once closely-knit, harmonious group had become a restless crew of disparate souls, some at odds with themselves as well as those around them, and though I realized this, I let it slide, thinking it would fix itself. Tricia Trent had left the year before, and with none of the old faces and allegiances around, that warm, close, trusting family we once had, it wasn't working. I was playing the right notes, but the piano was out of tune.

Gretchen even came on board to work with me for a year. She decided to take a break from teaching and try her hand at the agency business, and though this brought us closer together, after a while she realized advertising was not for her.

Having decided to leave the business for greener meadows, the time was appropriate to give a last hurrah for the dying relationship with her companion. Accordingly, she planned a lawn party for his birthday. One of his employees invited a friend that he knew from high school days. That friend was Stephen Marlowe. Now pause and consider this improbable scenario.

117

Here is Stephen in the midst of getting a divorce. Stephen meets Gretchen. Gretchen meets Stephen. At this point, you need to understand that the odds against the paths of these two people crossing in the normal course of events were astronomical. When they meet, it is love at first sight. I cannot put it any more plainly.

They wait until Stephen's divorce is final, and during the interim, I get to meet Stephen's parents who come to Greenville. Ron Levin—master marketeer, guru of strategies, performer par excellence, a legend in his own mind—meets Stephen's father, the Rev. Reuben B. Marlowe. A modest, quietly arrayed United Methodist minister of some forty-five-years standing, and at that time, pastor of "First Church" in Conway, South Carolina. The ground did not shake. No alarms sounded. No fanfare of trumpets. Just a get acquainted lunch with Reuben and his wife, Martha. I thought: Great. Now she's going to marry a minister's son. But that was fine with me: comparing this to the first marriage, it was going from the damnable to the divine.

As time passed, Reuben would come back up to Greenville, and after the marriage, he and I managed to go for a leisurely stroll or two, talking as any other two fathers might talk of their two children who had now become Mr. and Mrs. Naturally, Reuben wanted to find out about what I did, he thought it was very fascinating, but from my standpoint, I did not want to hear very much if anything about the church and God and Jesus Christ. What will I do if he starts preaching to me, I thought. It's like Gail Ressel all over again—old times come back to haunt me.

I had it half right. Something was coming to haunt me, but it was definitely not old times.

CHAPTER

16

In the early winter of '92, finding myself at odds with the world around me, still licking my wounds from the down-sizing, not being able to click, the lack of sufficient bookings, something began to take hold of me in a viselike grip. It left my mind quite clear, in fact, functioning better than ever, certainly on the creative level, and out of this funk or perhaps to combat it and deal with my anger and disappointment—I birthed one last giant, creative hurrah—a project that I thought was destined to take off like a rocket. With the help of an excellent illustrator, I had created a collection of fascinating caricatures with names and a funny copy story to match that would lend themselves to tee-shirts, mugs and so forth. They poked fun at politicians, politically correct people and others in our society, and everyone who saw the series said it was very, very funny. Breathtaking, they said. My greatest work. Absolutely.

Well, I thought to myself. I might have missed the boat with Miz Biskit twenty years earlier, but this time my ship had surely come in. Their enthusiasm piled on top of mine, and I funnelled money into the venture with unrestrained glee. This was the big one. The bonanza. Let other mere mortals pan for dust on their knees. I had reached down into the icy stream and come up with a nugget that would make me rich and famous. I had hit the mother-lode! To make matters worse, I was downing two hefty drinks every evening after work, followed by wine with dinner, and that followed by cognac with coffee and maybe just one more and then why not a little. . . .

Day after day, week after week, time all starts to run together, until there is neither beginning nor ending, and it's all a squirrel

119

cage in which the faster you run, the faster it goes. I wanted to slow down, but as the days passed, I felt more and more powerless to do so. My promises to change my life went up in smoke. Midsummer came, and after a couple of test rollouts, I realized we hadn't pulled the right trigger. Those people that saw the product loved it and bought it, but I couldn't get the distribution or exposure it needed. The political conventions were on, and one woman in Houston was so excited about the product, she got her friends to invest a small bundle to roll it out at the Republican convention, but the returns were fractional and disappointing. How could I have missed it? Me, the guy who *never* missed?

Reuben would come up to Greenville to see the kids, and one evening, after dinner at their house, he and I took a long walk in the deepening twilight. It must have been apparent to him that whoever and whatever had hold of me was eating a hole in my guts, devouring me piece by piece. By contrast, I sensed his quiet strength and deep compassion, as he would listen to my lament pouring out in a torrent. I must have seemed to him like a wild man, a freak from some neon carnival speaking in fragments of fire and light that shot out of me like skyrockets.

Explosion.

Sparks.

Darkness.

The next day he came over to the office, and we went downstairs into the think tank. The only sound was the muted hum of the air conditioner.

"Reuben . . ." the words wouldn't come. "Reuben, I want you to hear something that I read last night." I had the Bible open before me and began to read the 38th Psalm.

O LORD, do not rebuke me in your anger, or discipline me in your wrath. For your arrows have sunk into me, and your hand has come down on me. There is no soundness in my flesh because of your indignation; there is no health in my bones because of my sin. For my iniquities have gone over my head; they weigh like a burden too heavy for me. My wounds grow foul and fester because of my foolishness; I am utterly bowed down and prostrate; all day long I go around mourning. For my loins are filled with burning, and there is no soundness in my flesh. I am utterly spent and crushed; I groan because of the tumult of my heart. O Lord, all my longing is known to you; my sighing is not hidden from you. My heart throbs, my strength fails me; as for the light of my eyes — it also has gone from me. My friends and companions stand aloof from my affliction, and my neighbors stand far off. Those who seek my life lay their snares; those who seek to hurt me speak of ruin, and meditate treachery all day long.

I broke at this point and began to weep. Then I forced myself to go on.

But I am like the deaf, I do not hear; like the mute, who cannot speak. Truly, I am like one who does not hear, and in whose mouth is no retort. But it is for you, O LORD, that I wait; it is you, O LORD my God, who will answer. Or I pray, "Only do not let them rejoice over me, those who boast against me when my foot slips." For I am ready to fall, and my pain is ever with me. I confess my iniquity; I am sorry for my sin. Those who are my foes without cause are mighty, and many are those who hate me wrongfully. Those who render me evil for good are my adversaries because I follow after good. Do not forsake me, O LORD; O my God, do not be far from me; make haste to help me, O Lord, my salvation.

When I finished, we sat for a while in silence. My pain was his pain, my torment, his anguish, and I could see he was biting his lip to maintain composure and remain a source of strength for me. He did not try to "witness" to me, nor try to bring Jesus into the conversation. He didn't preach. He didn't lecture. He just sat there listening, sharing my pain. After I had gathered myself

121

together, he left to go back to Conway, and I faced the prospects of getting through another night.

I had started seeing a therapist whom I had known for fifteen years and for whom I had enormous respect. Slowly, he helped me retrace my steps back to my childhood and helped me to pick up the pieces and put them together. Just as with a puzzle, the best way to get started is to find the corner pieces then go on from there. That's what we did, and as a result, gradually a picture of why and how I had become the person I was began to emerge. It was not very pretty, but the truth about ourselves seldom is; and I knew it was time to deal with the whole truth and nothing but. Thoreau once said that whether "east, west, north or south, the ultimate frontier is wherever a man confronts a fact," and I had reached that boundary line without even being aware of it.

Yet, though I was gaining in self-understanding, emotionally I was still a shambles, and the feeling of dread would not go away. I had images that I was destined to die a lonely old man with pee-stained underwear, in a tiny rented room, heating soup on a hot plate—forgotten, ignored, unloved, a derelict. I actually believed that. The depression would be worse in the morning, and in the evening, I would sit in front of the TV until I was nearly brain dead. Anything to take my mind off the thought of having to wake up the next morning, for I knew that the minute I opened my eyes, I wanted it to be night again so I could escape through sleep. In the morning, I would thumb through the Old Testament, reading this or that, whatever caught my fancy. If you want to fill up time, try reading Leviticus. It's roughly akin to walking through Okefenokee with lead weights on, but it really didn't matter, since after a while the words all ran together like spaghetti. And then one night, I came across a passage in Deuteronomy that stopped me cold.

> Your life shall hang in doubt before you; night and day you shall be in dread, with no assurance of your life. Among those nations you shall find no ease, no resting place for the sole of your foot. There the LORD will give

you a trembling heart, failing eyes, and a languishing spirit. In the morning you shall say, "If only it were evening!" and at evening you shall say, "If only it were morning!" — because of the dread that your heart shall feel and the sights that your eyes shall see (Deut. 28:66-67).

I realized with a shock that this was exactly what I was going through. I read the passage over and over, thinking maybe I would find something in there to give me hope, but the writer seemed to be saying that if I didn't obey all of God's laws, He was going to come down on me and come down hard, but the more I resolved to change, to obey—the worse it got. I thought about the life I had lived and figured that now it was payback time as far as God was concerned. So what kind of hope was there for me? I didn't know. It was like being back in synagogue as a kid. God was this fearful, all-powerful, bushy-browed, bearded, scowling being who demanded absolute obedience to all these laws, and if you broke just one, you were in a whole lot of trouble. I was learning about who I was and who I was not, but there was no well of strength to dip into, nothing to get hold of. Therapy without confession and repentance cannot bring you out of the pit. Understanding *why* someone has stuck an ice pick in your heart does not stop the pain or bleeding. Someone has to *remove* the ice pick, in order for the healing to start.

I communicated my dilemma to my brothers, and their first concerns were not about my emotional health but rather my financial health. I had borrowed against the property, but at the same time, I still had the feeling there should have been a good bit more cash in the bank than there was, however I attributed all this to my state of mind. One brother came down to see me, then the other, both expressing dismay and shock, though each endeavored to be helpful and supportive. I'm sure the situation was almost as painful for them as it was for me, and in my state, I'm not sure that what I said made much sense.

The next week passed with my hardly seeing anyone, and I didn't get much down other than a little fruit juice and vodka. One morning, I looked at myself in the mirror and saw someone

I hardly recognized: pale, haggard, drawn, the eyes devoid of any luster, the face like a death mask. I stepped on the scale and saw that I had lost eleven pounds in five days. Perhaps it was cancer, I thought. Perhaps I'm dying and don't know it. I did not know how close to the truth that was.

Friday afternoon came, and there had been no one in the house with me for two days. No phone calls. No human contact. Just me and Josie, my standard poodle. She, too, sensed my mood and would come to me wanting affection, but look at me in a strange manner. When your own dog knows there's something wrong with you, it's time to hang it up.

I had no awareness of time other than suddenly noticing that dusk had turned into darkness, with no moon. The lights from the street shone eerily through the living room windows. I had not turned on the inside lights and found myself walking through the rooms in the dark as though I were searching for something, pacing back and forth like a caged animal. Finally, I went to my bedroom and sat down on the edge of the bed, burying my face in my hands. Josie came and lay down next to me on the floor.

Slowly, with no conscious effort on my part, as I sat there, the image of who I was began to take shape before me. Pieces of my past all coming together like different colored wisps of smoke. Apart from the financial considerations which were serious enough, apart from no longer having the exhilarating power of a going business, the recognition and approval from the seminars, the money—there was something else confronting me that was more terrifying than anything else. It was the fact that for a long time— perhaps longer than I wanted to admit, even *dared* to admit—I had been retreating into the cold, stark world of the inner-self, spiralling downward to a place so fearsome I did not dare to describe it.

All I knew was that at this very moment I felt caught in an avalanche—buried under ice in complete darkness and with only enough air to breathe to keep me alive. I could stretch forth my hand, but there was no one to take it. I was dying. Death was coming for me, and there was little I could do about it. You've heard of Chapter 13 and Chapter 11 and Chapter 7. I was Chapter

None. I was emotionally and spiritually bankrupt. Zero balance in whatever soul I might have once had.

I took out the Bible from the drawer of the nightstand, and as I did my hand fell upon the familiar profile of the Colt 45 that lay there beside it. As I sat in the chair humming a soundless tune, I wondered if perhaps this was the easiest way out. The simplest. I picked it up, then cocked it, staring at it intently. If I did what I was thinking, I would be invalidating everything I had ever done or been. It would be like having my soul stamped with the word *canceled* in big red letters. Then the real, final truth hit me: How could I kill myself? I was *already* dead and had been that way for longer than I wanted to admit. I put the gun back in the drawer and turning to the Psalms again, began to read, and that brought to mind how I had wept openly in the presence of Reuben only a few days before and how he had comforted me.

With his face coming hazily into mind, suddenly I punched in the buttons for his home in Conway and got a recording. I put down the phone and debated. Then I called Gretchen only to find out that Reuben and Martha were in Atlanta visiting their daughter, Deborah. Gretchen said, "Daddy, are you all right?" I told her yes, I was just exhausted and felt like talking to Reuben before I went to bed. That seemed to satisfy her, and I punched in the Atlanta number. Another machine, another message, this time from Deborah, his daughter.

I didn't need a machine.

I needed Reuben.

Now.

Now turned into five minutes, then ten minutes, then a half hour. The cold dread started to settle inside me again, this time worse than before. It was as though I were inside a car that had gone off a bridge and was sinking into an icy river, the water filling the inside of the car, displacing the oxygen, taking my life away a breath at a time. Suddenly I had the very strange sensation that someone . . . *something* was in the house with me. I got up to check all the doors, even downstairs, but they were all locked. Nonetheless, something was there. An indefinable presence— something rank and chilling. It smelled like death.

My death.

I went into the bathroom, locked the door and sat on the floor against the wall. Then it occurred to me that no door could keep out whatever demon it was who was after me, so I went back into the bedroom and sat on the bed. The one bright spot in my life–the one light that glowed steadily–was Gretchen, for it was she whose love I treasured and who had brought such joy into an otherwise tortured existence. She would be a mother in little more than a month, and with new life coming into our family, I wanted to live, but yet, I did not know how I could go on as I was. The thought of even one more sunrise was unbearable.

I sat motionless, hearing my breath coming in short gasps. My mouth was cotton. My arms and legs felt as though they were no longer connected to my body. I sensed the presence of evil, right there beside me, whispering to me under its breath, the sound of ragged claws scuttling across the floor coming toward me, something foul, something so hideous, so fearful I could not respond. I could feel it around my ankles, then climbing up my legs. . . .

Then, a funny kind of buzzing began in my ears, the kind that deaf people sometimes think they hear when actually they are hearing nothing. Then it changed in tone. I looked down at the phone and snatched up the receiver.

"Yes?"

"Ron, this is Reuben," said the familiar voice. "Talk to me."

For an instant, I had to make sure all this was real. That Reuben was really Reuben. That this was not one more trick of the senses.

"Reuben . . . I'm . . . I'm walking on the edge of the world." I began to cry softly. "I don't know if . . . I don't know what to do, Reuben. I just . . . don't know what to do."

"Ron, now listen to me." His voice was very even and measured. "You have a Bible there, don't you?" I told him I did, and he said, "Well then, pick it up, turn to Romans 7 and 8 and start reading."

"Romans? Seven and eight?"

"Yes. The book of Romans, Chapters 7 and 8." He spoke

very deliberately as though talking to a child.

"Just keep on reading until . . . well, until, you're so tired, you can't read anymore. I can't get away from here tonight because it's too late, but I'll call you first thing in the morning, or you call me, whoever wakes up first."

He made me promise to read just as he had said, then ended the conversation with a fervent prayer. I put down the receiver and opened the Bible to the book of Romans, something I knew only by name, found the chapter and began to read. As I began to read, the words of this man Paul struck sparks and began to catch fire with me.

> I do not understand my own actions. For I do not do what I want, but I do the very thing I hate. Now if I do what I do not want, I agree that the law is good. But in fact it is no longer I that do it, but sin that dwells within me. For I know that nothing good dwells within me, that is, in my flesh. I can will what is right, but I cannot do it. For I do not do the good I want, but the evil I do not want is what I do (Romans 7:15-19).

Yes, I thought. That's me. That's where I am. Someone actually understands. I kept reading as though in a trance, the words flooding into my brain like a tidal surge. This man and I had a lot in common. We both knew the same demons firsthand. And he was right. All the promises I had made to myself, I was incapable of keeping. I knew what was right, but I kept doing wrong. And even though I fought against the evil, I still wound up doing it.

The thought that another human being had struggled with this—a Jew, like me—let me know I was not alone anymore. That he understood.

> So I find it to be a law that when I want to do what is good, evil lies close at hand. For I delight in the law of God in my inmost self, but I see in my members another

law at war with the law of my mind, making me captive to the law of sin that dwells in my members. Wretched man that I am! Who will rescue me from this body of death? (Romans 7:21-25).

Yes, tell me, Lord. I want to know.

Thanks be to God through Jesus Christ our Lord! So then, with my mind I am a slave to the law of God, but with my flesh I am a slave to the law of sin. There is therefore now no condemnation for those who are in Christ Jesus. For the law of the Spirit of life in Christ Jesus has set you free from the law of sin and of death (Romans 8:2).

Then finally . . .

For those who live according to the flesh set their minds on the things of the flesh, but those who live according to the Spirit set their minds on the things of the Spirit. To set the mind on the flesh is death, but to set the mind on the Spirit is life and peace. For this reason the mind that is set on the flesh is hostile to God; it does not submit to God's law — indeed it cannot, and those who are in the flesh cannot please God (Romans 8:5-8).

I saw everything very clearly now. The truth was: the *law* in and of itself couldn't save anyone. The flesh is immune to that simply because no *law* can control the *flesh*. And this condition of humankind will always make me a slave to the law of sin.

Yes! My mind had been set on flesh for years: *flesh* meaning the material: that which I could taste, eat, touch, wear, grab, buy, spend, whatever. I couldn't stop reading. I turned back to the beginning of Romans and read the entire book. Then again. As I read and learned more about this man Paul, it became increasingly, *painfully* clear to me that the destroyer was the "I am" within me. I knew that I must surrender that to Christ, and if I did,

He would bear my sins away. He would take all that dead baggage I'd been carrying around for years: the filth, the pain, the bad dreams and bent desires, the wrong behavior that I had dragged behind me in a huge sack of guilt that had grown bigger and bigger, until I could no longer manage it. But now, I didn't have to any longer.

He would take it from me. Lift the yoke from my shoulders.

Through God's grace, His Son had died for *my* sin, though it was two thousand years ago. He had died to set me free so that I could *live in Him and Him within me.* The spirit came over me as I read, and the Word cleansed me. I fell back on the bed weeping tears of joy, exhausted, feeling my body go limp. I slept.

The next thing I knew I was sitting up in bed, my eyes blinking at the morning light streaming in through the windows. I felt different somehow. Wondrously alive. I leapt out of bed and turned to look at where I had slept and saw the indentation in the bed, a kind of hollow; and for one blinding instant, that I may never know again, I could see or I believe I saw an empty husk lying in the bed. A burned out shell. I knew as surely as I knew I was the son of Meyer Levin that during the night, there had been a death and a birth. A rebirth. Suddenly, I noticed the calligraphy from Deb that was hanging on the wall.

> *O Lord, Thou has searched me and known me.*
> *Even before there is a word on my tongue,*
> *Behold, O Lord, Thou dost know it all.*

Yes, God had known me all my life, though I had not known Him. Now, the circle was completed at last. I wanted to live with a passion and hunger I had never known before in my entire life. I knew who Jesus Christ was and why He had come, and why He had died for me. That I might live and serve Him in the kingdom on earth.

I was shaking so hard when I picked up the phone, I hit the wrong number. The next time I got it right, and Reuben answered.

"Reuben, this is Ron."

"Ron, how. . . ."

"Reuben, listen. Just listen to me. I want you to baptize me."

There was this moment of silence, then I heard him call out. "Martha, Martha! Pick up the phone. It's Ron. He . . . he knows the Lord! Hallelujah!"

CHAPTER

17

From that morning on, I became a different person than the Ron Levin I had known all my life. It was not any one single element of feeling or emotion that I could identify, but for openers, there was this indescribable feeling of peace within me. Joy poured forth from every fiber of my being. I have since learned that the strongest evidence of a transformation, an authentic conversion, is how one's behavior changes without one's even being consciously aware of it. And that's the way it was with me.

I was ravenous for the first time in weeks. I made a bowl of cold cereal with some trail mix, and a bagel with cream cheese, then realized I was still empty and drove to Hardee's and wolfed down two sausage biscuits—something I have never done before. And I was still hungry.

Things that once held my attention now had no interest for me. I all but stopped seeing movies. The TV stayed off. Magazines and newspapers piled up in a stack. The Bible and works of theology now became my sole reading fare, and I could not get enough. I read three or four hours every day.

Another gift came without my even being aware of it. About a week after my conversion, a longtime client and friend called on his car phone from Atlanta and said he'd heard about what had happened, and he couldn't wait to talk to me. "Hey, Ron, let's go down in the think tank and have some of that good stuff, just you and me." This man really liked his scotch. Then it occurred to me that I had not had a drink since that wonderful morning, and moreover, I had not even *thought* about it until he mentioned it. I told him I'd love to see him, and I'd have his favorite brand of

131

scotch waiting, but I wasn't drinking anymore. He asked why, and I told him. He was incredulous. He said he wanted to hear all about it, couldn't wait to see me and would call me the minute he got back into town. He never did.

Then there was the matter of my mouth. For as long as I can remember, since the age of sixteen, my language had been sprinkled liberally with profanity. Most men mistakenly think this makes them real macho, but from that morning on, I have never used the Lord's name in vain again, and all my former foul language has vanished. About the worst I say now is an occasional "hell," but mostly to make a point from the pulpit. As all this was happening, I paid a last visit to a client, the VP of marketing for a fifty-million-dollar company, for whom we had done a project or two. As I started to tell him what I was going to do, he shifted the conversation toward business; he was really wired that day because he had just gotten a huge order. As he talked excitedly from behind his gleaming desk, I became aware that every fourth or fifth word out of his mouth was godd- - - this or godd- - - that. He had always talked this way around me, as he did with everyone, but strangely enough, I had never noticed it before. Now, every time the words would leave his lips, I would actually wince. It was as though the words were darts that had been hurled at me, their points sticking in my body. I began to grow more and more uncomfortable, and I started to tell him, then realized he wouldn't understand. Finally, I thanked him for the work he had given us, told him good-bye and left.

My powers of memory and concentration, those gifts I had always enjoyed and benefited from but that atrophied, now started to come back to me. Previously, I would sit there in front of the computer and stare at the screen for long periods of time, nothing coming out of me, the wall full of awards for writing excellence of no avail. I had barely been able to write a page without forgetting where I was.

There was much more in me that was changed, but before I talk about it, I want to share the experience of my baptism with you. Reuben couldn't make up his mind whether I should be baptized at Buncombe Street or at his church, and finally he called, all on fire, and said for me to come on down the weekend of the 23rd. I arrived on Friday, August 21st and was baptized that Sunday morning. After-wards, Reuben asked me to give my testimony, and I got up in the pulpit and told my story from the top: just the way it had happened. I couldn't resist telling them how thirty-two years earlier, and ten miles away I had been playing in The Bowery and if someone had told me then that a generation later, I would be here in Conway First, newly baptized, witnessing to the power of Jesus Christ, I would have asked him what brand he was drinking and ordered him a double.

At a couple of times in my testimony, tears began streaming down my face, and by the time I finished, probably half the congregation were crying with me. I remember standing at the door being hugged by everyone who came out, and then two days later, I received a marvelous letter from Reuben's Minister of Music, Carter Breeze. I quote only a paragraph below:

> What a joy it was to have you here last Sunday, to meet you, and to share in your new pilgrimage in Christ, our Lord. How you captivated the people. As I sat in the choir loft looking out into the faces of the congregation, they were enthralled with not only you but with what you said. there was not a squirm, nor so it seemed, even a blink of the eye, as they sat there transformed by what you had to say. I have just finished rehearing the tape from the service, and I seemed to get even more from it the second time around. So, Ron, we celebrate with you ... we rejoice with you ... and we pray that God's richest blessings will be with you all the rest of your days.

I stopped by Trinity U.M.C. in Sumter that evening and gave an abbreviated version of what I had done in Conway, and the effect on the people was summed up by Reuben's son, Philip, in one word: electrifying.

When I returned to Greenville, about midway through the week, I decided to tell my good friend and art director, Mark Kelly, what I had done, and he broke into a broad grin.

133

"I knew *something* had happened to you, but I didn't know what," he said. "Now it all makes sense."

"What do you mean?"

"It's just that you're so different from the Ron Levin you were a week ago. The guy I've known for two years."

"Different how?"

"Well . . . for one thing, you're a lot more patient. Man, I cannot believe it. I went home and told Donna: 'Boy, something has happened to Ron, and it's like I don't know him.' It's . . . well, the way you always want things right now, gotta have them this instant, pound on the table—you're not like that anymore. You're not leaning on people every minute like you used to. I can hear this in the way you talk to suppliers on the phone. Man, you . . . ." He stopped, searching for the right words. "You're a lot easier to be around now."

I liked that. I *wanted* to be "easier" to be around. What was missing was the "lust" that we humans have, not in its sexual connotation but in the original meaning of the word, namely, wanting everything right now—this very instant, and whether or not our desire goes against God's will is of no consequence. Waiting may not be a virtue in and of itself, but I have come to realize that perhaps it is what God wants to accomplish in us *as* we wait. If I find myself waiting in line now, I use the time to pray or to think about others. Additionally, for too many years, I had enough carborundum in me to hone my competitive edge to razor sharpness, while simultaneously grinding others into fine metal shavings. Perhaps that best describes the final sin that with the help of my Lord, I have learned how to combat: the worst sin of all.

Intellectual pride.

The fact is: the sins of the flesh–those that far too many Christians get up in arms about–are little sins, for if you will recall Scripture, Jesus hung out with these people all the time and was very much at ease with them. In fact, He loved them though they indulged in what was regarded then as sinful behavior. What He had a far greater problem with were those people whose pride kept The Father at arm's length. One comes down with the virus of pride because one is richer than, better looking than, more talented than, smarter than—and so on. Pride is the mother of all sins, the one transgression from which everything else evolves. It alienates us from each other, then from our true selves, and finally, from God. It has been the death of more human relationships and joy than anything else we carry within us. And as someone once remarked, if you are *certain* you are not conceited, then you probably are. That's how tricky pride is. It is the great dissembler and masquerades itself in a variety of disguises, but once you have the indwelling Spirit, you are able to detect the sickeningly sweet smell of pride a block away and thus not be taken in.

What is most amazing is that none of these changes I have described came about by any conscious decision on my part to stop doing this or start doing that. They just happened, and I came to understand that is what is meant by the fruits of the Spirit, for when the Holy Spirit fills you, the harvest of joy and peace that you reap is bountiful beyond belief. A week or so later, I was driving on a quiet, residential street near my office when I suddenly burst into tears of joy and pulled over to the curb, sobbing over the wheel. A woman pulled up alongside me, honked her horn, rolled down her window and asked me if I were all right. Her face revealed her concern. I looked at her and laughed, saying, "Ma'am, I've never been better. Hallelujah!" I shouted. From the expression on her face, she could have just seen a ghost because she stomped on the accelerator and never looked back. I called Reuben and told him about it, and he laughed joyously. "Oh, Ron," he said, "you're filled with the Spirit, man. Isn't it glorious!"

It was indeed. By now, the word was getting around town, and people were calling from everywhere, and I was calling them. The first person I wanted to tell was Deb Dayhoff, and when she came on the phone and I told her, a long silence ensued, and I think she began to cry.

"Ron," she said. "I've been praying for you for years, ever since I met you, and now it's happened. God is so good to us, and He hears our prayers. He is going to do such wonderful things

135

through you, I know it."

Others called to congratulate me, and some even wanted to come over and talk to me. One well-known eminently successful businessman, a devout Christian, called me and said he had just heard about it and was in an important meeting, but he was going to break out of there and come over *right now* to hear my testimony; and lo and behold, within ten minutes he was at the door. As I walked him through everything, he sat there with eyes blazing. I was beginning to understand what Reuben had been saying all along: the actual, true-life story of how someone walks through a half-century of hell to get to Christ is more powerful than all the sermons that have ever been delivered. When I finished, the man said, "You know, of course, that you're Saul, don't you? Saul who became Paul. Instead of the road to Damascus, you took the back road to get to Jesus."

I said, "Yes, I know, I know!" He gave me a powerful hug, then left to share the good news with others. Of course, as soon as I could, I told by therapist about my conversion, but he knew even before I told him that something wonderful had happened to me. At our next session, he told me he didn't think he needed to see me anymore.

"You're going to be fine," he said. "You're in control of your life now, at least, the part that is yours, but more important, now you know that God has control over all the rest. You know how to move on from here, and best of all, you did it without any medicine." We shook hands and parted. What a wise and wonderful man he is.

On Monday around noon, Gretchen started having her labor pains, left school, got into the van, drove herself to the hospital and checked herself in. The next morning, September 15, Kathryn Anne Marlowe was born, and there was boundless joy over this beautiful, healthy child who had come into the world and into our hearts: Marlowe's, Levin's and our Lord Jesus Christ.

I had already begun going to church regularly with Gretchen and Stephen at Buncombe Street and often just sitting there, I would feel the presence of Christ beside me, the Spirit within, and my eyes would flood with tears of joy. After church one day, I wrote Reuben a letter saying that I wanted to become involved in the church, in ministry, but I wasn't sure exactly how. Reuben suggested that with my speaking ability and background, becoming a lay pastor would be easy enough to do. I could travel around speaking to various congregations. That sounded good to me, and I told him I would check into it. Then only a few days later, he called me and said, "Ron, I've been doing some thinking." I had been doing some thinking too, but I said, "You go first."

"Ron, with all your education and experiences and talent . . . ." Long pause and deep breath. "You need to go to seminary."

I said, "I know, Reuben. I've been thinking the same thing." We both gave out a whoop and holler, and the die was cast. I told him how I had felt the call to ministry growing stronger every day, until I could no longer deny it. He said it was too late to inquire about starting in January, and that I'd probably have to wait until next September, or summer at the earliest. I told him I didn't think the Lord wanted me to wait. Then the obvious question arose.

"Reuben, where should I apply?"

Well, for Reuben, that was a tough call. On the one hand, his youngest son, Jonathan, was a second-year student at Duke Divinity, but Reuben had received his Master of Divinity and doctoral degree from Candler School of Theology at Emory. "I don't know, " he said. "Try both."

It was Wednesday, September 30. I called Candler and was given to someone named Mary Lou Greenwood Boice, the Assistant Dean of Admissions. I gave her a one-minute biog of who I was and told her I wanted to come down to talk to her about coming to seminary in January. She said that she couldn't possibly see me for two weeks, but that I was certainly welcome to come down and tour the campus, but it was really too late to enroll for January . . . of course, there was always next summer and. . . .

I told her I was coming down tomorrow. I *had* to talk to her.

She demurred, and said politely but this time, a bit more firmly that she appreciated my sense of urgency but there was just no way she could make time for me in her schedule.

"I'm coming down anyway," I said.

"Ron Levin, you certainly are persistent." A pause. I could envision her checking her appointment book. "All right, but I can only give you thirty minutes and no more. Two o'clock."

I arrived the night before, then spent part of the morning chatting with a few students, all of whom were astounded that I, a Jew, with a career in business, had not only accepted Christ but was coming to seminary to be a minister. *And lo, the people were astonished.*

At two o'clock the next afternoon, I walked into Mary Lou's office and started in from the beginning. By the the time I got to that night in August, we were both in tears. She got up to get a tissue. She said, "You know, I've interviewed many candidates for seminary over the years, but yours is one of the most powerful testimonies I've ever heard. You're right, you're ready to come. I'm sure the transcripts and everything will be in order, but I would almost accept you without them." She smiled at that, and then said, "You'll be a brand plucked from the burning." I had no idea what she meant but I liked the sound of it. "Well, then," she said, "you'll start in January!"

I thanked her, glanced at my watch and couldn't believe my eyes. We had been talking for two hours. I had to get back to Greenville, and I couldn't wait to call Reuben; but at the same time, I had to get my act together because the clock was ticking, and in order to get ready for seminary, I was going to need all the help I could get.

The good news was—I knew just where to find it.

CHAPTER
18

Not everyone shared my enthusiasm.

My brothers were . . . well, I suppose the right word is dumbfounded. You must understand that for a Jew to take this step—to accept Jesus as one's personal Messiah—is the unthinkable. Something not to be talked about, discussed or even mentioned.

If you are a Christian reading this, you cannot begin to appreciate the upheaval this causes in the heart of one's family and fellow Jews. One very good Jewish friend in Greenville came to see me, and as I told her the story, she sat there, hands folded demurely in her lap, listening patiently. When I had finished, she smiled and said, "Well, that's all very interesting." She had no earthly concept of what I was talking about.

Later, another longtime Jewish friend said, "Listen, if it makes you happy, that's all that counts." I gave her C.S. Lewis' memorable line to the effect that "I didn't become a Christian to feel happy. I always knew drinking a bottle of good port would do that."

Still another, a Christian, remarked: "It's a shame you didn't do this five years earlier. Just think, you'd be that much far ahead." I told him that I wasn't ripe five years ago, and God knew it. If He had called me then, it would have been like pressing a marble instead of a grape. No juice. Nothing.

When God wants you, and His gentle nudges and subtle hints no longer work because you dig in your heels and refuse to be budged, He lets you sink all the way down to rock bottom, if necessary, in order for you to say yes. At that point, you either make a decision for Christ, or you will spend the rest of your days in torment so dreadful that no words can properly describe it.

The fact was: Jews simply did not do these things. In orthodox Jewish families, if and when this happens, the family actually goes into mourning, considering that person to be dead. I know an Episcopalian priest in a neighboring city who was born a Jew but accepted Christ while in college. His father did not speak to him from that day on, until he, the father, lay on his deathbed some twenty-two years later. This is unfortunate, and, I would hope, the exception. Jews and Christians have enough on their plate to deal with in the form, of say, a Louis Farrakhan and his insidious brand of venom, than trying to erect barriers between each other. Interestingly enough, one of the misconceptions commonly held among Jews is that to accept Christ, you have to give up something. You have to turn your back on your Jewish heritage. You don't give up anything.

You *get!*

Before I could go to school, there were some loose ends to be tied up, and Dick generously offered to help me refinance the property. Without this help from him, I could not have come to school. I was and remain so very grateful for that. At the same time, I knew my actions had to be a source of great discomfort to him, but I could not change what had happened. Through prayer, I was freed from dwelling upon this, but instead diverted all my energy and concentration to winding things down for my departure, starting with a garage sale, throwing out the junk and stuff that had accumulated over ten years. The two dempster dumpsters we filled were a good metaphor for the emotional and psychic garbage I had been lugging around with me all that time or longer.

I was now praying incessantly. You've heard of being paid up, I wanted to make sure I was *prayed* up, but from the start, I resolved I would not ask God for *things*, but simply for direction and strength. The first good news came in the form of my formal acceptance by Candler. I would actually be starting in January, and several days later Mary Lou called and notified me I would be receiving a partial scholarship.

Hallelujah!

140

We had a garage sale that was a great success. There would be enough for moving expenses, to pay living expenses for four months of seminary.

God Is Good!

I was ecstatic and Reuben cautioned me not to let my guard down. He said, "Remember what Paul said about putting on the whole armor of God. Just when things are going great, that's when you are most vulnerable, and for that reason, you need for your faith to be stronger than ever and be in constant prayer; for when things turn — and they will because Satan will not leave you alone — you will need to call upon the Lord for strength."

It didn't take very long. The next morning my accountant called and said he needed a check for $6,000 for social security taxes. He apologized for not having told me earlier and said it had nothing to do with salary (I hadn't drawn any) but it was because of the improvements made to the business property that now I had to declare as income. Surprise. My bookkeeper wrote out the check, I signed it, and just like that, my money for seminary was gone.

I kept on praying.

Christmas came, and I went to services at Buncombe Street and felt closer to God than ever before in my life, with an intimacy that made me feel *Yeshua* was standing next to me, sitting beside me, walking with me. Wherever I was, *He* was. The irony of this is that heretofore, December had always been the worst month of the year for me. Two times almost hit by a drunk driver: the first, a car crossing the median on I-385 and hurtling over the top of my car at sixty miles per hour just missing me by inches; the second, a year later almost to the day, a car that pulled out of an intersection in front of me, not a mile away from where the first incident had occurred. All this plus illness, business reverses, much more. Now my joy was limitless despite my concern about school.

Reuben was right: I would stay prayed up.

I also resolved to let Jack know what I was doing. We hadn't talked in a long time, but that had never bothered us before. Months would pass, but we always knew that the friendship and the love remained intact. His schedule was impossible, and one day he might be here, the next in New York, the day following in London and the day after — who knows? But just before I packed away my computer, I decided to send him a copy of my testimony, a ten-page capsule account of how all this had happened to me from day one. Rather than mail it, I had it delivered to his office then promptly forgot about it.

New Year's Day came, and I received another surprise. Laryngitis.

The movers were coming in three days. I had to be ready. But what about the house? Not to worry: the day after New Year's, someone came to lease it.

Everything is moving very fast now. We shift to present tense: the next morning the phone rings again. It's Candler. The money that I thought I was going to get is suddenly *not* available. Mary Lou expresses her regrets, and says perhaps I should think about delaying my coming. I tell her I'm coming tomorrow and the only way they can stop me is if the campus police bar me from entering my student apartment at Turner Village.

"I appreciate your determination, Ron, I really do."

"Thank you."

"I just wish there were something I could do, but my hands are tied."

"Mary Lou, I understand perfectly. I just want you to know that I'll be there tomorrow, and I appreciate all your help." I sit there with my eyes closed, talking to the Lord.

I call Reuben and tell him the bad news. He goes ballistic. His anger flows over the line like molten lava. "But they told you...I was assured...when you spoke to them earlier...I thought all this had been worked out...."

"Reuben, it's all right," I said. "I — " The phone rang again. I put Reuben on hold. It was Mary Lou. She said, "Ron, I have good news for you. Someone who was coming on a scholarship just canceled, and you *will* have a Dean's Grant for half of your tuition."

I thank her, hang up, get back to Reuben and tell him. Now the fury turns to astonishment, then silence. I hear him say, "God is good." We pray together, hang up, and I turn to wrapping up the last-minute details. The day passes by in a whirl of activity, and by six o'clock, I have finally gotten things in shape. The movers are coming in twelve hours. I still have a bed to sleep in, a bath to shower in, and a change of clothes, but that's it.

The phone rings.

"Hey, man, is all this stuff I'm hearing about you for real?" Jack!

I answered with a simple yes.

"Okay, I just needed to hear it from you. You let me know when you get down at school, if you need any help."

No words, just tears flooding my eyes. I tell him I will let him know and thank him. I sit there at the desk surrounded by boxes of every description. There is barely room to walk. I'm tired. Hungry. Worn out. And running on empty, the reserve tank already tapped out.

The phone rings. It's Reuben. I tell him the good news about the call from Jack. Reuben knew all about Jack and the California miracles, so he listens with great interest. As we are talking, the door opens....

In walks Jack and his wife, Anne.

"Reuben," I say, "you will not believe who just walked in the door," but rather than tell him, I hand the phone to Jack, and he and Reuben begin talking as though they were old friends, which, in a sense, they are. Jack and Anne stay and ask that I share my entire story with them, which I do. It is a powerful experience, for all of us. We say our good-byes with lots of hugs, and Jack's renewed commitment to help me in my mission.

Nothing has changed. God stays with God's people. That is the miracle of faith that is always there, just within reach. It is *we* who stray. So if you look around and suddenly notice that God is not there, then ask yourself this:

Who moved?

19

When I arrived at seminary, I felt like hanging a sign on my soul.

Under New Management.

However, the shock of reentry took some getting used to. First off, I went from a 2200-square-foot house to a 300-square-foot apartment. I missed my daughter; I missed my dog; I missed my friends. I had known and lived in one familiar environment and life-style for years, and now, it had been turned upside down.

Actually—make that *right side up.*

The tough part was finding how to go here, get that done, who to see for this, who to talk to for that, what to sign up for, what happens if you don't do this and so on. Now if you are twenty-five or thirty-five or even forty-five, it's not so bad. But when you are sixty, there is a difference. The saving grace was that in the midst of the crunch of getting under way, the confusion, the anxiety—God was never more than a prayer away, and if I was temporarily lost in my new surroundings, that was all right, for in my heart and my new life and my faith, I was *found.*

No matter what crisis or problem came along, I knew that we—the Lord and I—would be able to deal with it. And it did not take long in coming. I had signed up to take *Matthew* under Luke Timothy (there's a name for you) Johnson, a greatly respected New Testament scholar, and though my advisors put in a good word for me, Luke told me that the class was over-subscribed and there was no room for me. I had been reading constantly since my conversion in August, having already devoured some three dozen or so books, and I had learned enough to know that, as a Jewish Christian, I hungered to see Christ through the eyes of

Matthew who was writing to the Jews. I spoke to Luke in the hallway. He demurred.

I spoke to him coming out of the faculty dining hall. He left me with a polite, "We'll see." I buttonholed him in the corridor and said, "Listen man, I'll wash your car, cut your grass, whatever it takes, but I have to be in there." He laughed at that, checked the roster again and said, "Show up for class, and we'll see what we can do." I showed up, and the room was full, but I was in!

Luke is a cyclone that somehow manages to be contained in a classroom. The breadth of his scholarship is staggering, and combined with an irrepressible wit and a profound passion for teaching, the effect is having the synoptic gospels brought to blinding light. A lecture with Luke is roughly akin to eighty minutes of white water rafting. More important, and for me personally, this was my introduction to the person of Jesus: the times, the people, and the events that shaped history and changed the world. At first, it was all somewhat bewildering, but gradually, I began to understand, putting the pieces together into an intricate mosaic. It was an act of personal liberation through learning.

If you are a Jew reading these words, I can tell you that even if you came to Luke's classroom determined *not* to accept, understand or even *like* one single word of what you were about to hear—as told by Matthew, the Jewish tax collector and as illuminated by Luke Johnson—it is my conviction that by the end of the semester you would leave there profoundly changed in your attitude toward Christianity and Christ. We're not talking about *conversion* but rather conversation, which it is hoped will lead one to inner dialogue with the Son of Man, Jesus Christ.

Another class I had signed up for was suddenly canceled because the professor had been slightly injured in an auto accident. There didn't seem to be any other class at that time that made sense other than something called *Church Administration and Leadership*, taught by a Bishop James S. Thomas. I had no idea who he was, and neither did any of the students I asked. It

146

didn't sound very interesting—course descriptions seldom do, reading more like ingredients on a box of cake mix—but at that point, I was out of options. Consequently, I signed up and walked in that first Friday. Presently, a tall, elderly African-American man wearing a well-tailored three-piece dark suit came in, maneuvered his way behind the desk with the help of a three-pronged cane, and with a stately presence peered at us momentarily over his glasses. Then he cleared his throat and in a deep voice said: "Is this Church Administration and Leadership?"

We nodded.

He laughed. "I just want to make sure I'm where I'm supposed to be. You know, with the traffic so bad on the freeways, I have to pray myself to school every morning. I just get behind the wheel, and say, 'Holy Ghost, help me,' and . . . you know, all of a sudden I'm here." He gave out a laugh that was almost musical, we laughed with him, and that was my introduction to Bishop James S. Thomas. Though I did not realize it, he would shortly become one of the most powerful influences in my new life. The Bishop began by commenting on the weather, saying it was cold but not nearly so cold as Iowa where he had gone as Bishop (the first black bishop in the United Methodist Church) and in Iowa of all places, where in the mid-sixties, black folk were about as rare as beach umbrellas. He inquired casually if anyone else had lived in Iowa. I raised my hand and said that yes, I spent a year and a half in Iowa City where I had gotten my masters at the university, and I knew what he was talking about. Thus did Ron and the "Bishop" find their first point of reference on something as mundane as the weather.

January turned into February, winter came in earnest, the studying more intense, and mornings were harder to handle because I would read late with my eyes hanging out. Not only the required reading, but books of every kind about the Bible, theology, famous religious leaders, history and always Paul . . . Paul . . . Paul.

Classes began at eight. Still sipping coffee, a hundred of us would gather to hear Bishop William Cannon lecture on the history of American Methodism, as he would stroll back and

147

forth, sporting those delightful suspenders, tilting his head this way and that, looking up toward heaven as though to snatch the words right out of the air. His quicksilver mind and compelling narrative brought light into our midst even on those dreary, rainy mornings when gloom lay over the campus like a shroud. This man is a legend, and his life or vita needs no validation from me. I will say only that walking beside him through two-and-a-half centuries of Methodism was like having a personal guided tour in a format that computer people now call virtual reality. Of course, we realize that Bishop Cannon didn't *really* know John Wesley, Francis Asbury and all those other wonderful Methodists of the 18th and 19th century. Or did he? He made it sound as though it had happened the day before yesterday.

As the days passed, I continued to take great delight in the learning process, but there was something about seminary I did *not* like, and though I could not properly identify it, a vague sort of discontent began to set in like a storm front. Initially, I chalked it up to loneliness, and to be sure, part of it was. One night in desperation, I decided to find some female companionship. I went to the first cocktail lounge I could find on Cheshire Bridge Road, walked in, sat down at the bar and just as I ordered a grapefruit juice, an attractive woman came up and sat down beside me. She wore a stunning, low-cut red dress and before I could even say anything, she peered into my eyes and said, "For some reason, I feel compelled to tell you that I'm a witch, and I worship Satan. Now buy me a drink, and I'll tell you all about it."

I don't remember very much afterwards other than I managed to find my way back to the apartment in ten minutes flat, got inside, locked the door, went into my bedroom, fell on my knees and began to pray as though the earth were opening up beneath Turner Village. I asked God to forgive me, and He did. I prayed for strength of purpose, and I remained on my knees for a long time in quiet conversation with my Maker. I had been celibate since the August of my conversion, and as God is my witness, I have not broken that pledge, nor will I.

While there on my knees, my prayer concerns shifted to

school, and as I spoke and then would pause and listen, slowly the cause of my discontent began to unveil itself to me. For a long time, I had lived in a world where I was the leader: numero uno. I was the center of things, listened to and respected, always in charge. Here at seminary, it was exactly the reverse, and I realized this was what had been bothering me. But that was only part of it.

Certainly, any learning institution is a magnet for people with hidden agendas, and Candler School of Theology is no different from any other. Everywhere you turn, there's a cause or caucus trying to get off the ground. Bulletin boards are swamped in announcements. Buttons, badges, banners and balloons abound. But so what, I told myself. Maybe you're angry because it's not *your* cause. *Your* buttons. *Your* balloons. Because you're not the author, the creator, the founder, the emcee or your eminence or whatever. And as I continued praying, I realized that I didn't come here for any of that. My mission was not to earn a letter, a big "C" for Candler. I didn't come for a career. I'd already had one. I didn't really come driven to get a degree—I had two of those. And I didn't come to lead a movement or follow one—to have a badge pinned on me and pick up a trophy or a medal. I came because I was called. I came to deepen and strengthen my spirituality, and to understand and embrace the word of God so that I might better proclaim it to others. I had learned that *my* plan was of little importance when laid beside God's plan. Letting all this sink in, I remained kneeling for a long time, and when I finished, I realized that all of my anger and resentment had brought me that much *closer* to God.

Adversity teaches one the healing power of prayer. Weakness gives us an opportunity to become stronger through prayer. Anger is enveloped in God's love through prayer, and at that moment, I realized what Bishop Thomas had said the first day about praying himself to school.

I would pray myself through the days and challenges ahead.
Thank You, Lord. Message received.

From that moment on, seminary became a completely different experience. Concomitant with that, Bishop Thomas and I started to have conversations in the early morning before class. As we sat in his office and carried on our dialogue, I began to see more deeply into this man's heart, and what I saw and later heard in class, began to work wonders within me. One day, it was my turn to present my pastoral identity—a twenty-minute capsule version of my journey toward Christ—and when I finished, the class sat there not wanting to breathe or move. Afterwards, everyone came forward to hug me, some in tears. It was a powerful experience for all of us. A lot of these people had grown up in the church, literally, and my having them accompany me as I retraced the steps of my long journey home was as astounding for them as my pilgrimage to Christ had been for me. Afterwards the Bishop and I talked. He looked at me with those eyes that always seem to be on the verge of melting.

He said, "Mr. Levin, you need to be in a pulpit."

I said, "Yes, I know, Bishop. I enjoy my classes, but I didn't come just for that."

Now, I knew that to receive an appointment in your first year was rare, but especially so with someone like me who was brand-new to the church. I hadn't even been a Christian or a Methodist *for a year!* The truth was: I was so new I squeaked. It was no wonder, then, that people who were supposed to know these things had told me my chances of being given a church to serve were very slim. I shared all this with the Bishop, and we finished our conversation with his telling me to "wait for God's word."

March came and brought more bad weather. It also brought a call from the Methodist Center, and it appeared that a DS (District Superintendent for you non-Methodists) was inquiring about my availability to serve a church. They wouldn't tell me who, where or what. I told them yes, I was still interested, my heart skipping a beat. March 10th came. Dick's and Jack Stone's birthday. I returned from class to find a call on my answering machine. It was from Carolyn Morris, the Superintendent of Athens-Elberton, asking me to call her back. When I reached her, she said there was an opening in a small rural church about an hour from Candler—at a place called Between, and was I interested. A place called what, I thought, but she went on. Like all Methodist appointments, this one would begin in late June. She told me just enough about the church to pique my interest, and she said I could ride out there and look around, but "I was not to get out of my car or talk to anyone." I was to think about it and call her with an answer in a day or two. I jumped into my car and drove east on 78 toward Athens until I came to the sign: sure enough, it said Between. And there was a road called Ho Hum Hollow. *O Lord, I am slam dunk in the land of Canaan.*

Before I even reached the crossroads, I spied the church up on the left with the cemetery behind it. I turned left off the main highway, drove up in front of the church, pulled off the shoulder and got my first good look at New Hope United Methodist Church. The trees were gaunt, their limbs shorn of any leaves, and with a grey sky and the temperature falling, it was not the best day for a visit. Somehow, the church looked lonely. Forlorn. I sat there for a while then drove back into town, lost in thought. That night I called Reuben and told him about the opportunity. As usual, Reuben did not beat around the bush.

"Ron, if the Lord opens the door even a tiny crack, you jump through it!" I called the Bishop but couldn't get him. I prayed on it. And prayed. I was too excited to sleep well and awoke early in the morning, Thursday the 11th. I dressed hurriedly, gulped down a bowl of cereal and drove out to Between again. I parked across from the church and though it was quite cold, turned off the engine and sat there praying, enjoying the silence. A solitary, red pickup came down the road. When I finished praying, I knew what my answer was. I drove back to my apartment, called Carolyn and told her yes, and she was pleased at my decision. She told me I would move on June 24th and preach my first sermon on that Sunday, the 27th. Then I said to her, "I've been wondering about something. You haven't even met me, but you've given me this appointment. You must have a lot of confidence in me."

"Well . . . don't forget, Ron," she said. "God is in this, too."

It wasn't a rebuke, just a reminder.

I wanted to drive out to the church again to see it, but before I did anything it occurred to me I had forgotten to read today's devotional in *My Utmost for His Highest*–an extraordinary work of inspiration and guidance for the faith community, and there in the March 11 reading lay the following:

> Watch for the storms of God. The only way God plants His saints is through the whirlwind of His storms. Will you be proven to be an empty pod with no seed inside? That will depend on whether or not you are actually living in the light of the vision you have seen. Let God send you out through His storm, and don't go until He goes. If you select your own spot to be planted, you will prove yourself to be an unproductive, empty pod. However, if you allow God to plant you, you will "bear much fruit" (John 15:8).

The next day, March 12, I drove out for one last look, and as I sat there, the first snowflakes started to fall in what would be the biggest storm in years. A blizzard was about to blanket Atlanta. I drove back and once in my apartment, picked up Chambers again and turned to the passage: *The only way God plants His saints is through the whirlwind of His storms.*

I was about to be planted.

CHAPTER
20

I called everyone to share the good news with them. Depending upon who they were, the reactions were ones of astonishment, disbelief, joy or perhaps all of the above.

April came, with License to Preach School and final exams.

Reuben and I kept up a running conversation, and he would caution me to be on my guard. He didn't have to remind me, for I knew all about how the enemy attacks. And true to form, he did not disappoint us.

A call from my accountant revealed that the tax payment to the government had never been made. I said that he must be mistaken, for I had signed that $6,000 check back in December. He remembered and promised to look into it further. Without going into too many details at this point, a subsequent investigation with the help of my lawyer revealed that there was, in fact, a great deal more money that could not be properly accounted for, and my accountant informed me I would have to pay the government out of my own pocket. In one sense, I felt better since this helped explain what had happened to my business without my knowledge, but the far greater shock wave came just a few days later when a former employee took her life, leaving behind a grieving family and a lot of unanswered questions. I had met with her just three days before that and told her that whatever had happened, I still loved her and I forgave her. I remember relating this to someone, and his saying, "Boy, you really *are* a Christian."

I don't suppose we will ever know what happened or why, but I grieved for my friend, for she *was* my friend, and I prayed for the family she left behind. It was a devastating time for me.

Could I have saved her? When we had met, I had urged her to seek therapy and even told her I would pay for the initial sessions and did this in the presence of my attorney. I even gave her the name and number of Mr. Hart, who I knew would be able to help her. It was too late now. Her death shook me as nothing had in a long time and brought back recollections of how I had struggled with my own sense of worth almost a year earlier. By God's grace, I had been saved, yet tragically, and for reasons we may never know, she was lost to all of us who loved her. Lost forever.

During this time, a person whom I had met a month or so earlier was of enormous help and comfort to me. My meeting Diana Kennedy had to have been engineered by the Lord, for as with Gail Ressel, Al Batchelor, Jack, and all the other angels, the odds against this chance encounter were enormous. But meet we did, and as the friendship grew, Diana would come out to the apartment on those warm May afternoons, and we would talk for hours. She gave me Scott Peck's landmark work to read, *People of the Lie*, which confirmed my notions of consummate evil and experiences with Satan. For those readers unfamiliar with him, Dr. Peck is a world-renowned psychiatrist, and his approach to the subject of evil should keep you on the edge of your chair for a good many evenings. (I would love to say more, but this is not the time to do so. God willing, there will be other times, other books.) In any event, through my reading, prayers, and conversations with Diana, I groped for an answer that I could live with and slowly began coming to grips with the pain.

At this same time, a new project was launched, and perhaps more than anything, this helped to offset the tragedy that still lingered in my mind. It all began in this manner: during the semester, I had gleaned some choice morsels of wisdom and church lore from Bishop Thomas' lectures, though in actuality, they were not lectures at all, but more in the nature of illuminating conversations. One day, I told him we should do a book together. He did not think he was up to it, but I persisted until I had convinced him otherwise. We agreed to meet at his house for our first session, and when I arrived there, I found him fully prepared

154

with his pencils sharpened and a fresh, new legal pad laid out in front of him.

I said, "Bishop, we don't need any of that," and he looked puzzled. At that, I put my micro tape recorder on the card table, turned it on, picked up a thread from one of those memorable classroom "conversations" and we began. By the middle of June, we had done some twenty-thousand words, about halfway, but now we'd have to put it on hold, for soon I would be moving out to my appointment. Moreover, as the clock ticked down, I began to wonder how the people of New Hope would regard me, the son of a Russian Jewish immigrant, hardly the model for a United Methodist country preacher. Plus, I knew that they had been through a troubling episode themselves during the past year, and it occurred to me that both congregation and pastor qualified for the status of the "walking wounded."

I was due to meet with the outgoing pastor at a restaurant in Loganville called Charlie's on Friday, June 11th. I had a few questions about communion, and the pastor gladly agreed to answer these, and said we would be joined by a fellow minister and friend. As I headed east on 78, I began to feel a bit uneasy, but I couldn't identify the source of my discomfort. Surely I wasn't coming down with anything, was I? I had risen early and eaten a good breakfast, so I knew it couldn't be the hunger shakes. But as I continued on, whatever it was that had its hooks into me seemed to grow in its intensity.

Now as I relate what happened next, those of you who have not had a personal encounter with Satan may find all this mildly humorous, perhaps even ludicrous. That's your prerogative. I will not think the less of you, for your beliefs are your own—to live and die with. However, I would respectfully ask that you hear me out, then decide. In any event, as I neared Loganville, I began to hear a voice. I don't believe for a moment that you could have recorded it, but I heard it just the same. It went something like this:

155

*. . . You don't really think you're ready to pastor a
church, do you . . . these people won't like you at all . . .
they're gonna look at you and wonder if you're for real
. . . you'll be an abysmal failure as a preacher—the
laughingstock of the whole community . . . you're a joke,
boy . . . it's all a mistake. . . . go back to Greenville . . .
you're not wanted here. . . .*

By the time I got to the Ingles shopping center, I'd had
enough. Just after the KFC store, I jerked the Pontiac onto the
shoulder and stopped in a diving swerve, then leapt out, my arms
flailing as though I might have been swatting at a swarm of killer
bees. I began shouting at the top of my voice, and as best I can
remember, my words went something like this:

*"Satan, you're filth, you hear me! You piece of
garbage. You're vomit spewed up from hell. In the Name
of Jesus Christ and all the saints of heaven, I command
you to leave me alone. Now!"*

I stood there, sweating in the noonday heat, the cars whizzing
by, but I was barely conscious of them. I began praying, got back
in the car and kept right on praying until I got to Charlie's
restaurant. I'm sure I behaved a bit strangely during the meal, but
I hoped they didn't notice. I still felt the effects of what had
happened, but I could also feel the power of the Holy Spirit within
me. I knew I had to get inside the church as soon as possible, but
I didn't tell *them* that. Lunch seemed to take an eternity, and
finally when we had finished, we drove over to Between, some
six miles distant. I pulled up in front of the church, opened the
door and walked inside. I sat down and instantly, I felt the
quietude embrace me. Now I know why they call it a sanctuary.
At the same time, the memory of what had happened vanished as
though in a reverse time warp.

I knew with blessed assurance that this was where He wanted
to plant me. This was where I was meant to grow in His light and
love.

21

Love.

It is the force that brought a daybreak of hope to the hearts of the people—the single element that healed pastor and parishioners alike.

In twenty-five words or so, that's exactly what happened. And now that you've had the short version, I'll give you the long one.

I began by writing each church member a letter before I even got there. Bishop Thomas calls this "arriving before you arrive." When I finally did arrive on that Thursday afternoon, they were there to help me move in and get settled with welcoming hugs, food and flowers. Later came the honored Methodist tradition of "pounding," though instead of pounds of beans and grits and bacon, they gave me lettuce—the spending kind.

From day one, everyone at New Hope reached out to me with a love that was unconditional, unlimited and, amazingly enough, not tinged or tainted by what had transpired previously. The fact that they had been living with some hurts and bruises was something I already knew. (Face it: the same could be said about a good many churches in all denominations.) What they *didn't* know, however, was that their new pastor had experienced his share of the same—maybe worse. Then, with the coming of August and Homecoming, I began preaching in the elemental rhythms and furrows of the land that existed when King Cotton still occupied the throne. Afterwards, there was dinner on the grounds under a clear blue sky with tables of food reaching as far as a child could chunk a rock. Time to fill a plate, bend an ear, hug a body, shake a hand, tell a story, snap a picture and praise God from whom all blessings flow. Hallelujah!

Revival followed on the heels of this. People came from around the county to hear my story, and I stretched it out over three nights like a mini-series. To be authentic in our relationship, I knew I had to merge my story with theirs, and I held nothing back.

Nobody walked out. Nobody fainted. Folks didn't throw up their hands in fright. Oh, there were a few eyebrows raised, but from what I have read, the raising of eyebrows accompanied by grins, chuckles and assorted belly laughs has been going on ever since God stopped by for lunch one day and told Abraham that his ninety-year-old wife, Sarah, was going to have a baby. *Say what?*

I had even written a song for the occasion, and when we sang it in church, tears flowed freely. Everybody had come to see the new preacher, and I hope they weren't disappointed. Shucks, I'm six inches taller than Brother John was, and being as I could play the piano and sing like Brother Charles, I did just that on the second night of revival. I don't think anybody had seen a preacher at that church sit down and play and sing and carry on and such, and I hoped there wasn't anything in the *Book of Discipline* about that. My feeling about worship and church is this: joy first, rules second, God always!

As autumn came, my story continued to merge with theirs; and I discovered that the land and the people who inhabit it, whether Walton County, Williamston or Wilna, Russia, all share a common language. It is a litany of lost loves and missed chances, of hurts healed clean and others that have left scar tissue as a reminder. Opportunities that have come and gone like wind and weather. Memories that curl around the community and linger like the smell of wood smoke on a fall morning. Everything that ever happened winds up being a yarn in the pattern. Pull one thread, lose one life, and the pattern unravels at the seam of the heartland where land and sky come together.

As I spent time with the people, they began to open up and trust me. If nothing else, they could sense I came here to love them, not to change them. I came here to be a part of them, rather than apart *from* them. Thus, with the passing of time, I began to gain their trust and respect. One by one, their stories began to merge with mine, and a marvelous bond was being formed. Naturally, some folks are easier to get to know than others. Some are by nature private, others more open. It's all right: nobody's running a stopwatch. It's not a contest. Whatever can't be shared now will keep until later.

Log this away, please: I came to discover that on the very day that I was being baptized by Reuben in August of '92 at Conway, here at New Hope, some three-hundred miles distant, the church was undergoing a day of hurting that would shake its very foundations.

In the fall, classes resumed, and the regimen began in earnest. The morning drive into Atlanta is either thirty-two miles from here or a million miles away, depending on how one looks at things. Being a student pastor is not a piece of cake, but we were properly warned. Time tends to slip through one's fingers like sand, and if you don't cup your palms, it runs out in a heartbeat. Yet, "All things work together for good for those who love the Lord."

As autumn blended her palette then splashed the trees with color, my sermons began to change in much the same fashion. I had my hand on the pulse of life here, the rhythm of their voices, the furrows of brows and land, the songs of the earth. I had long since given up using notes when I preached. I also decided to get out from behind the pulpit—it's too much like a fortress. I want to talk *with* people, not preach *at* them. They've had enough authority figures in their lives telling them what to do, buy, vote, believe, think, drink, eat and wear. Anyway, authority is not something you command. It has to be given to you. And joy in worship is not something you can program or order from a computer menu. You either feel it or you don't. Louis Armstrong used to say, "It don't mean a thing if it ain't got that swing!" Faith is not a function of one's intelligence, breeding or income. It has nothing to do with the size of your car, your home or net worth, and these people know it.

Are there saints in our congregation? Well, not in the way the world thinks of saints, but I can tell you this. There are several

159

who come mighty close, but that's God's call. Not mine.

December came with a flurry of activity and childlike excitement. The Advent was a time of wonder, and we had a Christmas service that was as unassuming and modest as a manger. Folks said it was like the old-timey days, and I'd swap one comment like that for my Phi Beta Kappa key (which I can't seem to find anyway.)

Would that my old school chum, Charles Kuralt, could come here to see a slice of America that is becoming increasingly rare. Knowing Charles, the first thing he would want to know is the story behind the name Between. Some say it's because the town was halfway between Loganville and Monroe. Others because it's halfway between Atlanta and Athens. The best story of all is told by Metz Young who says that back during depression days, when someone asked why it was called Between, somebody said, "Because living here, you're halfway between hell and starvation." And from the stories I have heard, I reckon they were.

Here's just one of them: a family was once so short of food that when the winter swarms of blackbirds flew over their house, two young brothers ran outside and pointed shotguns up in the air, and dinner fell to the ground like manna on the Israelites. A passel of young'uns did the pluckin', and that night there were four-and-twenty blackbirds baked in a pie. *Now wasn't that a tasty dish to set before* . . . well, you know the rest. But what you *didn't* know is that this wasn't a nursery rhyme to fill their heads with fancy, but a survival tactic to fill their bellies before bedtime. End of story.

I promised myself before I began this book that for the most part I wouldn't talk about personalities or specific people in the church, but rather about the congregation as being the body of Christ in the purest sense of the word. Not just *pure*, but flesh, blood and bones as well. Hands that are strong, and some arthritic, the joints bent and out of order. Eyes that can see and some that are growing dim. Backs that are strong and some stooped and bent. Voices that sing out strong, and others that do well just to hum. Ears that strain to hear the choir but remain bent

160

to the ground of the community and perk up at the slightest sound of a cry for help. Legs that ache but belong to people who put feet on their prayers.

After a lifetime of harvesting tender moments and tough times, the people at New Hope have laid up a storehouse of simple, unadorned goodness in their hearts—those same values whose slow demise we are witnessing all around us. Dear reader, I pray you do not weep too long over the spotted owl or the snail darter, for the real endangered species are simple decency, honesty and caring. Like it or not, we are all part of America the beautiful, the battered, bruised, abused, badly bent and broke. We're one family, and as children of the Kingdom, we all have the same name.

God's love, like sunshine, falls upon all of us with His Amazing Grace.

The Blessing For Going Forth

What then shall we say about these things? If God is for us, who can be against us? (Romans 8:31).

The story of my journey is almost over.

I promised you in the beginning that I would present the case for a living God, and I have held to that covenant. Real people and real events embroidered on a tapestry that spans over a half century: a story of how God can work in our lives. Conversely, it is a tale of how some of us wind up going against the grain of the Kingdom through being stiff-necked, rebellious and resentful. The sad truth of modern life is that trapped in their spiritual bleakness, far too many people would rather walk ten miles to reject God's love than take one baby step toward the altar to receive it.

How do I know? How can I be so certain of this?

The answer is because I was one such person, and on my journey I met countless others. I still meet them today.

Now let us ask ourselves these questions.

Is it likely that a car can slam into a telephone pole at sixty miles an hour and the person in the front seat wake up without a scratch—still sitting in the seat? With an unbroken glass bottle of medicine beside him?

Is it mere coincidence that my father happens to sit next to Gene Stone on a plane and as a result, I meet his son, Jack, and come to work for Stone Manufacturing?

Is it not highly improbable that a tractor trailer parked in front of a McDonald's should lose its brakes, run down a hill some two-hundred feet, then leave the road at such a precise angle and place that heads it smack dab into Miz Biskit, thus demolishing my dream? (Had that come to fruition, who knows what might have happened to me?)

How is it that three years later, though we had not spoken in all that time, Jack calls me in October of 1974, an act which results in my going to California, a place where I had no intention of living? Not ever. Yet a place where I *did* go. A place where I was visited by angels.

Angels that bring God's message to us.

Consider Gail Ressel and the gift of prayer. Not once, not twice, but three times. I am looking for her, but cannot find her. (Gail, if you are reading this, please get in touch with me. We have much to talk about. God bless you.)

Angels that deliver God's gifts.

Consider Al Batchelor and the ten-thousand dollars. Is it likely that a retired postal clerk in 1977 in California would loan $10,000 to a relative stranger, recently moved there from South Carolina–a person who is all but bankrupt? On the basis of what you know about the person I was then, ask yourself this: Would you have loaned me the money? Tough call, huh?

Angels that intercede.

Consider Sal Salvatore and his last-minute change of heart and mind. What if he had forced me to go through with the transaction?

Angels that bring us God's word.

Consider Jason and Lisa, my next door neighbors, to whom God delivered me. They had prayed for God to send them a Jew for a neighbor so they could practice Christ's Great Commandment. Why did I buy *that* condominium in *that* place, when so many more were for sale?

Consider the fact that almost five years to the day after the call from Jack that took me to California, again he calls, and that results in my coming back to Greenville.

Consider my daughter, Gretchen. Is it coincidence that she goes to Charleston on a whim and meets "Ted" on a blind date. Ted returns to Greenville and hires "Bill."

A year passes, and Stephen Marlowe is invited to a party by Bill.

Gretchen meets Stephen.

I meet Reuben.

Then later, at the moment of crisis, Reuben introduces me to the Word. A Jew meets Jesus, as Saul did, and the Word brings me back to life.

God is good.

How have these things happened?

How is it that on the first morning I awaken after my conversion, everything about my behavior that was wrong and sinful and selfish falls away from me, like "scales from my eyes" with no conscious effort on my part?

How is it that after two months of trying to find someone to lease my car and the house, one man comes to take both, a man whose girlfriend is a Jewish Christian, her father a survivor of the Nazi death camps?

How do you explain that the money I had put away for school and just *knew* was safe had to be paid to the government instead? And how is it that at the same time, Candler calls and says their money won't be there? And then, at the eleventh hour, before the movers arrive, the money *is* there. How is it that after not seeing Jack for a year, he happens to be in town the night before I am scheduled to move—and comes over?

Is it coincidence that as I am talking to Reuben on the phone, telling him about Jack, he walks in the door?

How is it that I wind up in Bishop Thomas' class? It is certainly not what I had planned. The last thing I wanted. But through that act, I meet a man who is in sync with my soul as if he were my blood brother.

Angels abound:

How does Diana wind up in my life when she was given

165

every reason not to, and at a time when I would need a caring, trusting soul to bare my heart with only weeks later when the suicide occurred?

How is it that the third son of a Russian Jewish immigrant winds up preaching the gospel and proclaiming the Good News in a place called Between, Georgia? And this after having been a Christian and a United Methodist less than a year?

And as you have heard, how does it happen that on the same day that Reuben baptized me, August 23, 1992, in Conway, South Carolina, here some three-hundred miles away, in the community of Between, the congregation of New Hope endures a storm of hurt and the people cry out for healing? Whom will God send?

How could they know?
How could I know?
How could anyone know?
The answer is: we didn't.
God did.

Just as I have been called to the ministry, I have been called to tell this story of how God is using me and working His will through me. You should also understand that part of the miracle is the very writing of this book. I began it on December 10, 1993, and completed a finished draft in less than four weeks, some 59,000 words, on January 7, 1994. One year to the day that I came to seminary. Many people have asked me how I managed to do this, and I told them it was with the help of a ghost writer, and they said, "Ah hah, we knew it." Then I told them, "The *Holy* Ghost." And they became silent and went away and pondered these things.

For my family and relatives who may ponder these things, I can only tell them that I am a living tree planted beside the waters, with the roots of Abraham and the branches of *Yeshua*—the anointed one. He who saves. Jesus the Christ.

Let us consider I Corinthians 13:4-7 . . .

Love is patient; love is kind; love is not envious or boastful or arrogant or rude. It does not insist on its own

166

way; it is not irritable or resentful; it does not rejoice in wrongdoing, but rejoices in the truth. It bears all things, believes all things, hopes all things, endures all things.

For those readers who knew my father, Meyer Levin, you must also know that he lived his life in this exact manner. For those who did not know him, please understand that even though he had never read these words, nonetheless, they were written on his heart. In a land where we came as aliens, he was loved and embraced by all. On those strolls through his beautiful orchards in the cool of dusk, did he perhaps walk alongside the Messiah. Was his a different kind of road to Emmaus? He never talked about things of this nature, but always kept such matters to himself. Did he want to tell us something, but didn't know how? That perhaps he knew *Yeshua* in a way that did not lend itself to words. In light of how God has acted in my life, may we not, then, consider such a possibility?

Would we be offended?

Would we be shocked?

Would it diminish our father in our eyes?

Oh, I think not.

It did not shame Saul, the Jewish tentmaker from Tarsus. It gave him new life, as it did to me on that August morning, and what, then, shall we make of Saul? Was he lukewarm about his faith and heritage? Was it all tangential and peripheral? Was it fantasy? Fiction? Consider the facts:

Saul grew up in a Jewish family in Tarsus, still a thriving city not far from the Mediterranean on the southern shore of Turkey. He was well trained in Jewish Scripture, and at an early age, he entered the synagogue day school and learned to read and write through copying the ancient Scripture. He learned Greek, and he also learned the art of tentmaking. When he was in his early to mid-teens, he went to Jerusalem to study under the renowned rabbi, Gamaliel, who was the grandson of the greatest rabbi of them all, Hillel. What does Paul himself have to say about all this?

167

If anyone else has reason to be confident in the flesh, I have more: circumcised on the eighth day, a member of the people of Israel, of the tribe of Benjamin, a Hebrew born of Hebrews; as to the law, a Pharisee; as to zeal, a persecutor of the church; as to righteousness under the law, blameless. Yet whatever gains I had, these I have come to regard as loss because of Christ. More than that, I regard everything as loss because of the surpassing value of knowing Christ Jesus my Lord. For his sake I have suffered the loss of all things, and I regard them as rubbish, in order that I may gain Christ and be found in him, not having a righteousness of my own that comes from the law, but one that comes through faith in Christ, the righteousness from God based on faith (Philippians 3:5-9).

In much the same manner that the scales fell from Saul's eyes and he became Paul and was reborn, it happened to me. Or do we think that miracles only happen once and never again? Is that what we want to believe? If we accept the miracles in the Old Testament, then can we not accept those in the New Testament as well? And if we accept those, then can we not say that miracles still occur today? Or did they end at some fixed point in time?

Was the book on miracles closed?
Did the offer expire, never to be repeated?
If there is a living God, then surely His work is without end.

"What then shall we say about these things?"
I have said what I came to these pages to say. Now it is for you to decide. If you believe that all of the events and people are happenstance, mere coincidence, so be it. But can all of them be just that? What if only three were done by the hand of God? What if two?
What if only one?
What, then, shall we say about these things?
That is your decision.

168

I already made mine on that great gettin' up morning in August.

"So if anyone is in Christ, there is a new creation: everything old has passed away; see, everything has become new!" (2 Corinthians 5:17).

Here am I, Lord: a rough sawn roustabout hewn from the same Joshua tree as Paul.

Where do I go from here?

What has God planned for me?

What will He ask me to do?

I have no answers for these questions.

Yet, in the midst of the hurly-burly of my life, the crucible of challenge, days of testing and trial yet to come—I know that wherever He leads me, I will trust and obey, and one simple truth will be my rod and my staff.

The Lord is my shepherd; I shall not want.

THE END

In Honor of my Mother, Minerva Finzimer Levin

Your love for us was as fierce as a blast furnace,
we boys cast like fine steel in the mold of your
and Meyer's making. Naturally, you expected us to
shoot the moon and scrawl our names across the sky
big as life. And naturally, we gave it our best shot.

I was the baby the doctors warned you not to have.
No more, they said. But then, what mere physician
could possibly know more than Minerva.

Now, the slow creep of time has engraved your face
like the rings of a live oak growing, too stubborn to yield
to wind and weather. And though age and arteries have
dulled that once keen edge we marveled at, your bag of
knitting still hides mysteries beyond our wildest imagining.

Dear Mother, for too long, I was held prisoner in the
depths of a river I could not fathom. Then one morning,
surprised by joy I swam upward toward sunlight and broke
the surface in sight of shore. Standing there, the Messiah
beckoned me, with loaves and fishes on every hand.

Rejoice! Your baby boy is anchored by the roots of
Abraham but this time with the branches of Christ, all
bearing the fruit of the Spirit . . . *ruach!*

It's me, mom. The last to leave your body.
The first to know our Lord.

Transition

*I wrote this immediately after visiting with my mother in a
nursing home in March of '94. On the evening of November 15,
later that same year, Mother left this world, but not before I had
a chance to visit with her again. I know that Meyer and Minerva
are together. And if you are curious about just how I know, write
me and I will surely respond. Hallelujah and Amen!*

171